Find Your Pink Flamingos

Celebrating the Gifts of a Mom

BY DEE DEE RAAP

Reader Reviews

"I loved Dear Mom, but I love Find Your Pink Flamingos even more! What a superb job of capturing the emotional journey of finding the gifts of our moms...thank you!"

Amy Engel

"Dee Dee and her writings first sparked my willingness and then became the guiding light when I gained the courage to look for the gifts I received from Mom, Dad and others who have defined my life. Find Your Pink Flamingos gave me so many 'aha!' moments I need to go back and re-read it so I can capture those moments and experience others. Thank you, Dee Dee, for showing me the way."

Mary Cerney

"Plain and simple—Dee Dee's a gifted writer who makes an emotional impact. Her heartfelt stories in both Dear Mom *and* Find Your Pink Flamingos *make me smile, laugh, cry and appreciate my own 'Dear Mom.' Dee Dee delivers hope and healing, real gifts from a writer who helps us celebrate the gifts from our moms."*

Nancy Monson

"Dee Dee's message on finding the gifts of a mother's love is in itself a gift to those who are grieving this loss. She provides necessary tools for using memories to sustain the relationship beyond life. This approach offers an ongoing comfort and peace when experiencing the journey of grief. As she speaks to grieving people she reinforces the tremendous gifts that are received from mothers, 'hidden' in words and actions so easily taken for granted. I encourage readers to enjoy Dee Dee's newest book, Find Your Pink Flamingos, *to treasure the memories and appreciate a mother's love forever."*

Dr. Marcie R. Moran

Dedication

To the loving memory of my aunt Bernice,
my "other mother,"
whose 92 years on this earth
just wasn't quite enough.

Thanks for teaching me to be strong,
trust God, and to enjoy the journey.

Thanks for a lifetime of love!

Disclaimer:
The information contained in this book is intended for general reference
purposes only. It is not a substitute for professional advice. Guidelines
and strategies are meant to acquaint you with procedures currently
available and the manner in which they can be carried out.

Edited by Caron B. Goode
Layout by Jessica Raap Johnson
Book cover design by Jessica Raap Johnson
Printed and bound by QQP

Published by JW Press
4015 S. Brady Ct.
Sioux Falls, SD 57103
605-371-2299
DeeDeeRaap.com

About the Author

Dee Dee Raap is an author, motivational speaker and business consultant with 25 years of experience working in media, travel, banking and marketing. Dee Dee founded JourneyWorks, a speaking and business consulting firm, in 1996, and since then, has spoken to groups across America on communication, customer service, teamwork and leadership.

Dee Dee's passion is helping people find and live the values that help them excel personally and professionally, what she calls "Making the journey great!" She is passionate about helping organizations create values-based cultures that build loyalty with customers, employees and members. She is the author of several books, an ezine and numerous articles on service and leadership.

Dee Dee is a Distinguished Toastmaster, member of the National Speakers Association and a community volunteer. She lives in Sioux Falls, South Dakota.

For more information on speaking engagements, special discounts for bulk purchases or for personally signed gift copies of *Find Your Pink Flamingos*, please contact Dee Dee at:

Dee Dee Raap
4015 S. Brady Court
Sioux Falls, SD 57103
605-371-2299
deedee@deedeeraap.com
www.deedeeraap.com

Acknowledgments

My journey as an author is the result of many people whose faith in me far exceeded my own. Thanks to my husband, Kim, who believed in Flamingos from the very first time I shared the idea. Thanks to my friends whose support encourages me to keep telling my stories. Mary, Diane, Vanda, Vernon, Mrg, Virg, Reneé and Jim....your compassionate friendship results in many acts of kindness that have made a very real difference in my life. Thank you.

My journey as a mom, mother-in-law and a "Gumma" to little Faith and Gavin has taught me more than any book. The stories of life with each of you is a journey that has filled my cup with blessings I could never even imagined possible. Thank you.

Since writing and publishing *Dear Mom* five years ago, I have met thousands of women and men who have shared the journey of transforming loss into the journey of finding the gifts of the one they lost. Your courage, your faith, and your words of encouragement and gratitude have been all the reward I could have ever sought for a journey I didn't plan to take.

My life has changed for the better because of all of you. Thank you. It continues to be a wonderful journey!

Table of Contents

Foreword

GIFTS FROM THE HEART

Values are something we assign high worth to in life. Their imprint is lifelong, and like the rudder of a ship, they steer our life course. Sometimes, we disconnect from our values, or we take them for granted, or we stray from them, or we behave in ways that contradict them. Dee Dee's book gently reminds us to be conscious of the gifts our moms share with us through the values they imparted.

As a mother and grandmother, I am an expert in declaring mothers are not perfect. Yet, I have always been intrigued with the word "imperfection." One can read it as imperfection or "I-m-perfection." That is what mothers are, imperfectly perfect! And Dee Dee captures this in her book. Not only does she capture it, but it is the pulse of her book.

Her beautiful message to us is to see, appreciate and pay forward the blooms our mothers have offered us throughout their lives. Yes, there are weeds and perhaps even a few thistles, but there are so many gifts from mom. Dee Dee captures them in beautiful and distinct ways as she talks about the values our moms imparted to us.

She demonstrates repeatedly, through stories, her own and others, how important it is to realize the legacy inherent in valuing optimism, humor, and simplicity. What a great way to greet each day! What a different day it is when we meet our challenges with optimism, when we can laugh at ourselves or the preposterousness of something gone "so" wrong; or when we can simplify and enjoy the precious gifts each day offers. When we value simplicity, we remove the clutter in our heads and in our lives, and we are better able to appreciate our relationships, the little moments that form the very best memories.

How do we come to know the inner royalties of living from a place of compassion and kindness? I like to call this heart-centered living. Where would we have learned it is safe to open our hearts if not from our mothers? Granted some moms have an unusual way of showing their compassion. They could look and sound tough on the outside, but when they sacrifice their time to help someone in need, or push through their fatigue to offer support to those who have none, these are the "poignant and real moments."

We use to call my mom "Sarge." She was bossy and uncompromising. But let something happen to someone who needed help, and she used that same energy to support that person through the crisis. She was not much interested in compliments or recognition, but she did make sure that my sister and I learned how important caring and compassion were to living a full life.

Dee Dee shares some wonderful stories about faith and gratitude. I recently read a card that said, "The only transportation around here is a leap of faith." What else helps us move through our losses and grief? What else helps us believe in tomorrow? What else allows us to see, despite our pain, the beauty in each and every day? As Dee Dee says in her book, "I think seeing the best in people is the closest we come to being angels while we're here on earth."

To be able to see beauty even when we are hurting, is a mom gift and it has an angelic quality!

When my mom was dying I asked her to send me a signal that she had arrived "on the other side" and was safe and in a good place. My mom responded, "I'll try but I don't know if I will be able to do that."

Shortly after she passed, I returned home with my youngest daughter. We were both feeling deeply sad and so we were silent. I opened my bedroom window to let the spring air come in. My daughter followed me into my bedroom, and both of us heard a double train whistle. We looked at each other, shocked because there are no train tracks anywhere in the vicinity in which I live. My daughter and I smiled at each other and we instantly knew, "Mom was okay. She was in heaven." She did figure out how to signal us and we got it.

That very moment remains with me daily. My mom passed seven years ago, and I mostly remember with deep gratitude her train whistle; and my next thought is one filled with deep gratitude not just for her signal, but for her life. For all the things she wanted for my sister and me; for all the sacrifices she made for us; for all the times she yelled at us to make us better human beings; for the high expectations she held for us to ensure we could take care of ourselves in life and offer a hand to those in need.

Dee Dee's book is deeply touching. You cannot read it without shedding a few tears and a few smiles and giggles. Through her wisdom and stories, Dee Dee reminds us of what is important in life, what matters, and what gifts we need to remember and celebrate because they were given to us in unique ways by our moms, and they help define who we are today.

Elaine K. Williams, ACSW, CHt

Author of *The Sacred Work of Grandparents Raising Their Grandchildren,* Balboa Press, Autumn, 2011.

Introduction

The time was the late 1950s, when Americans settled into a prosperous era of productivity and invention on a national scale. Families formed into communities...around church, education, neighborhoods, and farms. Families took pride in their homes and properties, convinced that colorful flower beds and green lawns needed some colorful decorations.

GOOFY FLAMINGOS

Even on the South Dakota prairie, home to ducks, geese, and pheasants, my mom was convinced that one more bird would add even more beauty. In front of her ranch-style house, my mother, Betty Hauge, moved in a flock...a whole flock of pink flamingos. These plastic creatures lived on the green lawn in front of her aqua house. She even installed a white picket fence in front of them. I wondered back then if she thought they were going anywhere.

Mom embarrassed me with her pink flamingos! You have to understand this situation through my child eyes that saw the farm north of Roslyn, South Dakota as a wildlife paradise of hills, sloughs and trees, home to deer, geese, ducks, swans, mud hens, muskrats and more. On a busy day, five or six cars, maybe 10 cars on Sundays, went down the gravel road that was about 50 yards from our house. But every time a car drove down the road, I blushed. I just knew the people in the car saw the pink flamingos. They knew we were goofy and silly to have fake birds. Oh, how hard I tried to hide the fact that we were goofy!

FLAMINGO FLOCKING

Flamingos have gone from a few select sightings in the 50s and 60s to becoming a cultural icon in America. "Flocking," the practice of sneaking an entire flock of plastic pink flamingos onto a front yard during the darkness of night, has become an effective fund raising tool as well as a way of celebrating significant birthdays. Madison, WI, had its capital grounds flocked in honor of Wisconsin proclaiming the pink flamingo as its state bird. However, my personal favorite now is seeing flamingos in gardens and yards, standing tall amidst flowers and bushes, as if protecting, watching over, or guiding. In fact, flamingos can be sighted almost everywhere!

A cultural icon has become a personal symbol for me of the values that guide my life. I once thought Mom's gifts included things she made like the Christmas ornaments that adorn my tree each year. Now I see that her gifts were the extraordinary values she taught in a very ordinary life on a farm, and as with the flamingos, I now see her gifts everywhere.

SETTING THE STAGE

For people like me with rural roots, life doesn't get much better than waking up on a farm. Horses whinny, morning doves coo and the corn stands tall—all greeting a prairie sunrise that inspires the most talented artists.

I feel at home when I wake up on a farm. The feeling is familiar because I spent the first 15 years of my life on a prairie farm with cattle and chickens, farmers with tractors who planted and harvested fields, and a mom who planted and harvested a garden every year.

I didn't appreciate the gift of growing up on a farm. The grass was always greener someplace else, known as "the other side of the fence" to us farm kids. Even cattle knew grass was better on the other side. Why else would they jump a fence and create the repetitive chore called "chasing cattle" when the prairie was green—or brown—on both sides of the barbed wire?

Growing up on a prairie farm during the turbulent 60s disallowed a dream I had from age 14. I wanted to be a hippie. I wanted to march for civil rights and against the war and the establishment that seemed to not care. I wanted my voice to join the millions of others not yet called The Baby Boom Generation. I wanted to make a real difference out there, where the action was, on the other side of the fence.

It was easy to take the prairie life for granted. It was so quiet and there was not much action on the prairie, after all. As black and white television showed the civil rights demonstrations in the early 60s, the prairie seemed far removed from the headline news each night.

Yes, this was reality…I was on a farm with fences, and I had an older brother who thought rock music was a bad influence. So I grew up listening to Hank Williams Sr., Ernest Tubb, Hank Snow and Buck Owens. I knew the words to *Tiger by the Tail* and *Your Cheatin' Heart* before I knew the words to any of the Beatles' songs.

FAST FORWARD

Fast forward four decades later and I'm enjoying the quiet farm country. I feel at home in a place I had taken for granted during the first 15 years of my life. The first time I appreciated the prairie was when I brought Kim, my fiancé, home from college to meet my family and see where I grew up. Kim stood on the land I called home and said, "It's so beautiful." Beautiful was not a word I had used to describe the dusty farm, but I began to see the rolling hills and tall prairie grasses through his eyes.

The second time I appreciated what I grew up with was when Mom died. Losing her suddenly with no chance to say goodbye or thank you made me realize how much I'd taken for granted all those years on that prairie I had called home.

The gifts from my mother's life—those amazing values that guide my journey—were hidden in love and life lessons. Like the flamingos, I had to look at them twice to find Mom's gifts to me in the ordinary life of an ordinary woman on the prairie.

Now her legacy stands out, like the flamingo, tall and proud, pointing the way with that long neck and beautiful beak.

FLAMINGO FANTASIA

And there begins my story of finding the gifts of Mom's life, hidden in birds whose plastic bodies stood on metal legs, brightly accenting a prairie I love, where the gifts of my mother's life shaped my own.

When I was writing the letters to Mom in what became the book *Dear Mom*, I wrote one in Mexico when I saw real flamingos, and I asked Mom why she had them. Then I found the answer. She was doing what every mom did, trying to make the environment a little better. The prairie can be hot, and heat can make it dry. She wanted to add color and a little sense of humor. That's my theory. My brother says she got the flamingos on sale at the dime store in town and couldn't resist a good deal!

That's it…. the pink flamingos have become the metaphor for the values I didn't know I had received from Mom.

Now, just like finding more gifts of my mother's words, actions and traditions, there are pink flamingos everywhere…. my aunt and uncle found a "flock" in Nebraska and brought them to my home. Despite my daughter's embarrassment, they adorn my lawn and symbolize the gifts of my mother's life.

My flamingos have helped me celebrate my gifts from Mom every day. I have photos of one of my flamingos wearing a red scarf for the American Heart Association Go Red Campaign. I have a photo of her standing proudly in front of the American flag one day in a Toastmasters meeting. She has entertained my granddaughter, embarrassed my daughter, and become the state bird of Wisconsin. No wonder she wore a cheese head when the Green Bay Packers won Super Bowl 45.

A WONDERFUL LIFE

"Each man's life touches so many other lives," counseled Clarence, the guardian angel to Jimmy Stewart's character George Bailey in the classic, *It's a Wonderful Life*.

In my version of wonderful lives, I believe that each mom's life touches many other lives.

I published my first book, *Dear Mom, Remembering, Celebrating, Healing*, in 2005 because I knew that it would help people who had lost their moms. I knew the incredible pain of losing my mom suddenly without the closure of saying goodbye. The years it took for me to heal finally started one Christmas and has continued as I reach out to help others bring closure to their loss.

Losing a mom is one of the hardest things you'll ever face. The journey of remembering and celebrating is one of the most important you'll ever take. For that reason, I believed God inspired those healing letters to be published in a book, and I finally got it done. We all deserve wonderful lives filled with love and appreciation.

I've been blessed to meet many people who have shared stories of their moms, and I've collected amazing cards, letters and e-mails from readers of *Dear Mom*. The heart-warming feedback from a community of women and some men, who understand that the loss of a mom is a very significant life shift in life no matter one's age, has been an incredible part of my journey of celebrating.

One day during a speech, I found myself telling an audience that the values I got from Mom were her real gifts to me. Realizing that the core, personal values are the essence of our goodness—our ability to serve, to make a difference, to be our best every day—was my breakthrough moment. My inspiration rose like an eagle taking flight. Suddenly, I was sharing those values in book events, and then in presentations to women's groups, and then through keynotes. Eventually, Mom's values became a part of my customer service training to a high-tech telecommunications business in South Dakota.

I now see the valuable, unending circle of a mother's gifts passing through generations simply by the way we live our lives as families. What I cherish from my mother I have passed to my daughters. Since I have become a grandmother, I observe how my daughter shares what she received with her own children, and how her sister conveys similar messages as an aunt. Our values become the glue that holds us together.

PAY IT FORWARD

What we pay forward are the values our mothers or some other wonderful persons gave us at an early age. Those values are rock-solid foundations of our character traits. I see such values shared with others in the goodness of people, their acts of kindness, compassion, and forgiveness. I see them in creativity and resourcefulness, and in humor and cooperation.

My goal is to help you find the gifts of your own "Dear Mom," or other people who were key to your life when you were a child. I'm passionate about helping everyone be the best they can be, because they already are! They already have it in them. It may be very cleverly disguised, it may be buried deep or just below the surface, but this I know: your mother put it there, and no one can take it away.

Perhaps the journey of healing from the death of our moms gives us permission to live life more fully, for we see how life and death are entwined. Yes, we will all die, but the real questions are:

- Will we live fully and passionately?
- Will we help and serve where we can?
- Will we celebrate all we have been given?
- Will we choose daily to be fully present to the gifts of the one who gave us life?

I will! The reason is because thirty-five years ago, I made a simple decision that proved to be prophetic in my life. I chose my wedding announcement with silver calligraphy on aqua blue paper, with Kahlil Gibran's simple words that have come so true: *"Love joins our present with the past and the future."*

I believe it's a journey worth taking because of the gifts you'll find: the love, the life lessons and the legacy of values. Real values—not some version of values that can be bought or sold or are promoted for self-indulgence, but genuine, authentic values that can only be lived and shared!

SECTION ONE

The Journey

"One day you finally knew what you had to do,
and began…."
Mary Oliver, The Journey

How amazing is your life journey? Do you have great adventures filled with wonderful days of brilliant sunshine, the giggles of small children playing delightfully, and time spent with people you love and cherish? On some days, every road you take seems to be a smooth, straight path to your destination.

Then there are other days when the sun doesn't shine, and the journey becomes hard and lonely. Days when every road is filled with potholes and you stumble into nearly every one. Days when the road has confusing detours that slow your progress.

Life is a journey of paradoxes that offers both kinds of days…sunny and not sunny, smooth roads or detours. Life is like that. The yin and the yang, the opposites producing what we didn't expect and could never have predicted.

The hardest journey of my entire life started with the day my mother died. Yet, some of my greatest joys came from the healing from her death.

THE DAY LIFE CHANGED FOREVER

In December 1990, I was 34 years old and enjoying having it all. I had two beautiful daughters, a wonderful husband, the fulfilling career at South Dakota Tourism, and volunteer positions in school, church and Girl Scouts. Why wouldn't I have been extremely busy? My generation believed that we could do it all. Moreover, we would do it all well.

Yet, being busy wasn't enough for a tried and true female can-do-to-all Baby Boomer. My husband, Kim, and I also decided to tackle remodeling the kitchen. On December 5, 1990, our kitchen was stripped down to bare walls. The living room was filled with the new cupboards in large boxes, and our bedroom served as the makeshift kitchen. In the middle of this mess, the phone rang. On the line was my sister who urgently said, "The hospital called. They don't think Mom's going to make it. Get home now!" Click.

Stunned, I called her right back, and she repeated her message. I sat, doubly stunned, on the bucket of mud, the only chair available in the middle of the makeshift kitchen.

DEALING WITH DEATH

I have wondered why Mom died at the most hectic time right before Christmas when I was in the middle of remodeling a kitchen. But, now I realize we have little say about the timing of events on the journey. Things happen, stuff happens, and what matters is how we deal with it.

I dealt with Mom's death by going into shock. I lost seven pounds in seven days, but had no clue that I'd lost weight until a friend took me shopping. Whoa…I was fitting into a size I'd never worn before.

I felt like a time bomb was slowly ticking within me as I saw people enjoying Christmas, saw lights and decorations and felt a horrible emptiness inside. The bomb exploded on Christmas Eve during church services as I sobbed. I had buried my mom, and I hated that the rest of the world was celebrating the holiday she had created every year of my entire life—until this year.

I dealt with it by going to counseling, denying, getting mad at God, pretending to be better, figuring out that wouldn't work, and slowly working my way through the grieving process.

I grieved, yet my journey back to life as the busy Baby Boomer continued with two small daughters, my career, and my husband. We moved to another house. I made six more trips to Japan for South Dakota Tourism, changed jobs, and in 1996 we relocated to Wyoming for my husband's work.

COMING TO TERMS

In 1999, I finally dealt with Mom's passing on December 5, the anniversary of her death. Mom's simple Christmas ornaments, crafted out of red, green and white yarn, sometimes blue, decorated my tree each year. She skillfully made miniature mailboxes with the year, bird feeders, stars, even a miniature church that reminded of me of Fron Lutheran Church where both Mom and Dad are buried near my hometown.

That day, I sat on the couch, enjoying a cup of coffee and looking at the ornaments, when I began to see them as "gifts" from Mom. That made me think of other gifts from her, and question what I would say to her if she were still alive. That was so easy to answer. I would tell her about Jessica, Kelsey, Kim and me.

At that very moment, an inner voice said, "Get up off the couch and go downstairs to the computer." For a change, I listened to that little voice and went to my computer. I sat impatiently, finally looked up over my left shoulder and said, "Now what?" My hands responded and simply wrote, "Dear Mom." My fingers swiftly typed an emotional outpouring. I bawled a flood of tears, releasing pent-up grief that I never imagined was balled up in me. Then I wrote "Dear Mom" again, and I cried and laughed as the second letter poured out. Thereafter, I kept writing, feeling lighter with each missive.

Over the course of six or seven months, I wrote more than 70 letters about simple, ordinary things like the first day of snow, Valentine's Day, Mom and Dad's anniversary, my birthday, Easter, spring, and how her granddaughters were growing. The list went on. Words flowed so easily on to the computer screen, sometimes on a napkin in Mexico, and once on a piece of scrap paper in a Cody, Wyoming hotel room. Wherever I was, whatever happened in my life became a chance to have another conversation with Mom. I asked her questions I might have asked had I known our time together would be so short. I found the answers in my writing.

Mostly, the letters gave me an opportunity to express my gratitude for all Mom had done, said and given me. The hardest thing about sudden death is being robbed of the chance to express love and gratitude. I have seen others lose a loved one with the time to show their love through hugs, tender words of thanks, and sharing memories of wonderful times that allowed both to smile and give thanks to the Maker of the journey.

THE THANK YOU CARD CALLED "DEAR MOM"

Something nearly magical, certainly spiritual, happens deep inside of us when we give thanks. Our gratitude fills emptiness when we acknowledge all we have received, and we celebrate it by giving thanks. This highest form of prayer demonstrates how blessed we are to see what we have, instead of what we have lost, to focus on the good instead of the bad.

I never had closure with Mom. I never got to tell her thanks for all she had done for me. As I wrote letters continuously, *Dear Mom* became one big thank you card to Mom. My joy is that many people used the book to write letters of thanks to their moms. One woman wrote her mom letters, placed them in the book, and gave it to her mom for Christmas. Others tucked their own letters inside of the *Dear Mom* book to gift the moms for Mother's Day presents. Many have told me that my speaking to them about the gifts of their moms prompted them to make that phone call they'd put off. Those stories describe the beauty of their journeys. Finding the gifts of our mothers' lives is good for us; it's good for our mothers, and it's good for those who follow us.

The journey is finding—remembering—giving thanks—and celebrating—the gifts of the one who gave us life.

That incredibly ordinary woman from the incredibly ordinary prairie of northeastern South Dakota gave me more than I ever realized. When I finally said thanks to Mom, I experienced the healing I needed.

God inspired my way of dealing with Mom's death. I didn't write the letters to write a book, but thanks to encouragement from friends and family, I published *Dear Mom: Remembering, Celebrating, Healing* five years later. The journey of self-publishing could be called "Do it yourself project—with support and a great editor." I found my editor, who loved the subtitle, because, she said, "So many people think they have to heal before they can remember and celebrate. You're telling them they can remember and celebrate, and that will lead to healing."

I wrote to heal. I call it narrative healing because writing was my medium; my writing narrated my memories of Mom and healing was the wondrous result! A journalist called me an accidental author because I wrote without intending to publish. I wrote letters to Mom in a random process, inspired by dishes, weather, events and celebrations that brought to mind another question for Mom, or another story that had to emerge from within me onto the piece of paper or napkin or notebook. Writing to Mom was an emotional release that continued for more than 70 letters.

"Every time an old person dies, it's like a library burning down."
Alex Haley

After publishing *Dear Mom*, inspiration pushed me to continue writing. I wanted to stay in touch with the amazing women and men who shared my journey. I decided to publish for the past five years a *Dear Mom E-Letter* in which I have shared stories about healing from the loss of a mom by finding the gifts of her values.

Sharing my healing stories was risky for me. I work as a professional speaker and consultant on matters related to customer service, communication, leadership and life balance—not on the topic of losing a mom. Sharing such a personal journey was never on my list of professional goals. I didn't plan to work with hospice and bereavement counselors. I didn't plan on having book signings and presentations in which audience members were in tears. And I didn't plan on receiving a file full of cards, letters and notes thanking me for what I shared. Sharing was simply something I knew I had to do. The rewarding responses affirmed my decision to take the risk of publishing *Dear Mom* and continuing to share my heart in my *Dear Mom E-Letters*.

Letters and e-mails from readers of both *Dear Mom* and my *Dear Mom E-Letters* have blessed me.

"As my mother's life narrows to my house and her bedroom and bathroom, with occasional forays into the sunlight in my den, I watch her quietly and let my heart feel the love I always wanted us to share. We never had matching dresses, like my friends and their mothers; we never became best friends or shared secrets and hugs. But I have this time of caring for my mother in a loving, compassionate way and I am so blessed."

"I've been grieving for over a week and I have no control over what's about to happen. I feel helpless. Thank you for letting me know that grieving is OK. Your 'Dear Mom Letters' are a blessing."

"I wonder - how many of us have been 'helped to heal' from our Mother's deaths, through you? Just the other day, in 'tidying up' for Christmas, I ran across a letter I'd written to my mom.

Mom died in August (I don't even remember what year - it doesn't matter - it could have been this very past August or ten years ago!) and this letter was dated just days before Thanksgiving - - - In it, I'd written about my phone calls to her regarding 'the bird,' and whatever else I was making for Thanksgiving - talking about mashed potatoes - - - you know - - - the things of life that make/made memories.

I was not sitting on my porch reading it; I was sitting in that 'then' kitchen I wrote from, with Mom across the table from me - well, actually - I could see her kitchen. I am ever so grateful I wrote that letter, and kept it.

Thank you, Dee Dee, for what you do for me, and the hundreds & thousands, like me - and you :)"

"Dee Dee - Once again you touched my heart ... my father's name was Orvie and he served in World War II ... I could just imagine what his Mother's Day card would have said to his mother. This being the first Mother's Day without my mom, it is bittersweet, as I know where she is. Thanks again for your Dear Mom letters, they are such a joy."

"My mom always thought decorating our family graves on Memorial Day was extremely important. After she died I kept that tradition alive. Every year, my sister and I go to the cemetery in Lake Preston and put flowers (NOT PLASTIC) on the graves. Mom hated plastic flowers!!

And then I read that you take water and wash off the bird poop on the gravestones. I started laughing and so did my sister. She has made fun of me for years because I always take water and a sponge AND a broom to clean everything off before we set flowers on the graves. Now I know I'm not the only one doing that.

Thank you for sending the 'letters' to me. I enjoy each and every one of them."

"The newsletters are wonderful and are an exceptional gift to those who are seeking healing after the death of a loved one."

"My grandmother called Memorial Day, 'Decoration Day,' and that was because they always visited the cemetery to tend and decorate graves of the family members who have passed. I have 'been there, done that,' as you described in your letter. Knowing that your story is closely connected to mine is what provides the healing. To know that we humans are all connected and not separate is the key, I think, to everything in life."

This letter in particular makes such a true statement about all of our hearts and our pains. None of us is alone, even when we feel solitary and sad after the death of a mom or dad. We forget in our overwhelming heartache that every human being has, is or will experience the same burdened heart in death.

"Years ago I met you while you were in Cheyenne, and I purchased your 'Dear Mom' book. At the time Mom was a survivor of her first cancer -- Colorectal. Three years ago when my mom was diagnosed with her second cancer - Endometrial, I re-read your book and started writing my own 'Dear Mom' letters. Sometimes they were short and sweet -- like the one I scribbled down on a receipt as my daughter made our traditional Christmas cookie. Others were literally pages and pages -- like the one that came after I dropped my oldest off at college last fall. I will never be able to share in words how much these letters meant to both of us. She must have told me 100 times how much she appreciated 'getting to know me with words.'

"Mom's funeral was yesterday and we spent the weekend starting to go thru her home in Illinois of 30+ years, and I came across the stacks of pages I had sent her. They were in her night stand and they were tattered and torn like a well-loved book. I have no doubt Mom read them over and over. So, I wanted to thank you! You started this journey for me with your loving, inspirational book. THANK YOU!"

TAKING GIFTS FOR GRANTED

"Being taken for granted can be a compliment. It means that you've become a comfortable, trusted element in another person's life."
Dr. Joyce Brothers

Familiarity may be the reason we take for granted the people who are most important to us. Stay-at-home moms raised many Baby Boomers. Mom's presence in life was natural and assumed. We didn't know what day care meant, and we rarely had baby sitters. Preschool didn't exist on the prairie and neither did kindergarten. I was home with Mom until first grade.

I loved school. My teachers were wonderful women with names like Mrs. Lardy, Mrs. Roth and Mrs. Gruby. Eventually, I had Mr. Glad and Mr. Pereboom. They were my teachers for language, arts, history, bookkeeping and typing. Dated myself quite nicely with that list, didn't I?

However, Mom was the teacher of life, and a sneaky one at that. She taught what I really needed to know without telling me I was being taught lessons for life. Mom's best teaching technique was repetition in words, actions and traditions. In other words, she was consistent in her words and actions. She was a model of integrity.

Mom taught me compassion, kindness, and patience by being so. For example, she exhibited great patience during the many times I announced at bedtime that I needed a pan of brownies for school the next day. She always baked them.

It was Mom who taught me honesty, trust and optimism. When I complained about a problem in school, Mom would say, "There's a silver lining in every cloud." When I was sad over breaking up with a boyfriend, Mom said, "There's always more fish in the ocean." (Really, Mom? Thought we lived on the prairie…)

She taught me to have a sense of humor, to treat others the way I would want to be treated, to always give my best effort to anything I did. One of my jobs was to dust. When I took shortcuts, Mom would say, "If you're going to bother doing something, do it well."

Mom modeled lessons on compassion, kindness and patience, plus other timeless, authentic values were instilled in those growing up years. I simply saw her in action, taking care of her father, allowing strangers stuck in a blizzard to make our home theirs until the storm subsided. I saw hospitality without ever hearing the word.

She repeated key phrases. "Do it right the first time." "Hard work never killed anybody." "Close the door, were you raised in a barn?" I memorized those phrases because I heard them so often. I simply thought it was part of her job. Mine was to listen and take appropriate action.

In addition to being Baby Boomers whose mothers were usually home, we were also raised by what Tom Brokaw coined America's Greatest Generation.

AMERICA'S GREATEST GENERATION

> *"...But taken as a whole this generation did have a 'rendezvous with destiny' that went well beyond the outsized expectations..."*
> Tom Brokaw

Our nation's most senior members are survivors. As kids they survived the Great Depression, the Dust Bowl and as young adults, they survived fighting in and supporting WWII. They lived with a sense of sincere gratitude for life with rain for crops, food for family and cattle, and plenty of gasoline and sugar—both rationed during WWII.

My family members of that generation—Mom, Dad, my

aunts and uncles—had been raised by a very modest breed of people who believed that telling their stories constituted bragging. Discovering the stories of my parents' generation has led to finding the gifts of their values—the core values that helped them survive struggles of epic proportions.

I discovered the story of my great-grandmother who homesteaded as a widow with two small children. The gifts of that story were perseverance, hard work, and strength. I discovered that Mom had been a schoolteacher, and then quit when she married Dad. The gifts of that story were loyalty, compassion, hard work and a love for family. I'll never forget the night my dad told me for the first time stories related to WWII and how he earned three Bronze Stars and the Purple Heart. The gifts of that story were understanding the sacrifice young men made for our freedom—and the fact that few of us had any real clue as to what they endured fighting in the Pacific Rim.

I value the stories that hold the values of life that strengthen us for the journey and share them with my daughters and my grandchildren. I believe our lives are enhanced when we authentically live these core, personal values to the best of our abilities. The examples from our past do a great job of guiding us with courage into the future.

COURAGE

We can find the values of our parents, grandparents, aunts and uncles through conversations and videos, letters and life reviews. My late aunt Bernice is a great example. She lived to be 92, played poker three times a week and she played to win. I loved hearing her stories of the flour sack dress, finding favorite antiques, life growing up in South Dakota and her mother's life in Olso. I love knowing I am related to her because of her strength. Her strong genes are mine, and her courage offers an example of strength that I can choose. After all, she said it many times: "Be strong."

My journey of discovering profound courage in the lives of my mom and other women in my family happened by asking them to help me, guide me, and to be there for my children and grandchildren. It's a wonderful way to make my journey great.

Death is a very intimate journey for the living. Most recently, my aunt Bernice died. Those of us who knew her deemed her passing a bit premature. After all, she was still living alone, playing poker and making plans for attending her home church's 125th anniversary.

I spent the night in Bernice's hospice room in Minneapolis. Just before returning home to Sioux Falls the next day, I was alone with her. I held her hand and stroked her hair. With each stroke, I said, "thank you, for..." My list went on and on as tears flowed, my heart heavy with loss, but very grateful for one more night with this woman who had been in my life forever.

I can only imagine the journey of the one who has passed on, how they must smile when they look down. I know Mom smiled the day I said thanks. And I'm sure she said, "She got it!" That's how powerful the healing journey is.... the journey of remembering and celebrating the gifts of the one you've lost.

It's a journey I highly recommend you take.

HOW TO USE THIS BOOK FOR YOUR JOURNEY

There are three places where you'll find the gifts of your mother's life, and section two of this book will guide you through the process.

- First, you'll find the gifts of your mom in what she said. Did you hear your mother say, "Count your blessings," when you complained about not having what your friends had? I did, and her words taught me to be grateful for what I had, even though I really wanted something else.

- Second, you'll find gifts in what she did. Her actions most likely spoke volumes. Did your mom always make room for others at the dining room table? Mine did. And it taught me the value of heartfelt hospitality.
- Third, and my favorite, you'll find your mom's gifts in honored traditions and unique items like plastic pink flamingos Mom had in her prairie yard in the 1960s.

Section Three will help you see the spiritual heritage you received and show you some ways of "paying it forward" to your children and grandchildren. Finally, you'll find a meditation I wrote to guide you to have "one more day" with your mom.

Finding the gifts of your mom's life is a very pro-active journey of discovering, not blaming. When you find behaviors, words or actions that hurt or confuse you, let them go, like holding them tightly in your hand, and then gently opening your hand and watching the wind blow them away. Forgiveness is not only divine; it's part of what helps us heal. Why would you take junk with you on your journey? Have courage to let go and forgive, and replace what didn't work with what does work.

My daughters are examples of courage in action. Aunt Bernice told both of my daughters to "be strong" at tough times in each of their lives. Bernice knew how hard it was to be a young mom with a husband off to war. She knew the struggles of tough times. So did my mom. Both Bernice and Mom offer real examples of strong women who made do, created what they needed from what they had on hand, and faced each day being the best they could be.

My prayer for my daughters and my grandchildren is always strength to deal with whatever life throws at them. We all suffer loss—of loved ones, of things that won't happen as we'd hoped and planned. Trusting God, your Higher Power or whatever you believe in, is a way of acknowledging we're not in control, and we don't have to be.

What we have to be is open to the experience, to life.
The best way I know to do that is to trust God.

One day, when my Aunt Bernice and I were driving across the prairie near our hometown, I asked her how she did it. How did she stay so strong in her life, given the fact that she survived the Great Depression, lost her husband, lost my dad to whom she was very close, and lost her mom? She looked at me and said, "Two words: trust God."

This I now know: I have fewer days ahead of me on this journey than I have behind me. I will not waste my time blaming, criticizing, or condemning. I will relax, enjoy, celebrate, cope, survive and thrive to the best of my ability every day. With a lot of help from God, I will daily live the serenity prayer: accept what I cannot change—other people, and change what I can—me, and have the wisdom to know the difference.

That wisdom makes the rest of my journey great. But in the accepting part, I can also accept the best of the gifts, tucked away in stories that illustrate the values I hold dear. And when I accept the gifts of those who have gone before me, I am changed, able to better live in the strength of those values. And that makes my journey great.

SECTION TWO

The Gifts

MOM'S LEGACY OF VALUES

*"I am blessed by remembering and celebrating
the best gifts of my mother's life—
the love, life lessons and legacy of values
that make my journey great."*
Dee Dee Raap

Some people have dogs. Some people love cats. However, I have a flock of pink flamingos, a strange tendency I inherited from my mother. In section two, you'll discover a very true fact that could brighten your day or make you terribly sad. The true fact is that we women become like our mothers. Love or hate your mom, but embrace your mom's legacy with humor, love, and if needed, a sprinkle of forgiveness for her gifts to you.

My story of Mom's legacy became apparent to me in July 2004 when my husband, Kim, and I moved from Cheyenne to Sioux Falls before I completed the book *Dear Mom*. I believe the move was God's way of giving me the time to grieve my dad's death, as well as propel me to finish the book *Dear Mom*. I spent the year missing my dad and writing about my mom, and my heart was raw and vulnerable and grateful.

Our daughter, Kelsey, stayed in Cheyenne and worked at a restaurant to help pay for college. She took the indirect route back to college in Spokane by first coming east to Sioux Falls for a two-week visit. When Kelsey got out of her car, she first picked up the pair of plastic pink flamingos in my front yard and moved them into the back yard. Apparently Kelsey did not appreciate my flamingo humor, and she was a bit embarrassed by her mother.

As she unpacked her suitcase, Kelsey said, "Mom, your friends at the restaurant have been asking about you, wanting to know how your book is coming along. Then they complimented me. Guess what they said? 'Kelsey, you are so like your mom.'"

I could tell by the look on her face and the tone of her voice that the she wanted to scream. Kelsey looked me in the eye, insuring I received her message: "I'm going to scream if one more person calls me 'Little Dee Dee!'"

Ah yes, we do become our moms. I smiled and with a twinkle in my eye, replied, "It's like this, Kelsey. Mirror, mirror on the wall, you've become your mother after all!" I have to commend Kelsey. She exercised considerable self-restraint, especially when I kept smiling and gave her pink flamingo Christmas lights to cheer her up.

We really do become our mothers after all. The really good news? We can choose to become the best of them by taking the journey of finding the values they instilled in us. We just need to remember and celebrate that fact. The stories and questions in this section help you take that journey.

So I remember Mom, and my symbol for her gifts to me has become my pink flamingo, and a whole flock lives in my front yard. Sorry Kelsey! You can relax…the neighbors are used to it.

FINDING YOUR OWN PINK FLAMINGOS

Yes, I have a flock of flamingos. I have bought some, but mostly friends and complete strangers who have shared the journey called "Dear Mom" have given them to me. I have a stuffed flamingo three feet tall and one that is only one foot tall. I have pink flamingo Christmas tree lights and two large Christmas tins decorated with flamingos wearing Santa hats. I have flamingo napkins, toothpicks and a pen given to me by a friend who saw it in a gift shop in Florida, and said it was, "Screamin' Dee Dee!"

I have flamingo notepads, a flamingo journal, flamingo candles, puzzles and cards. I have a Vegas showgirl flamingo and several flamingo Christmas tree ornaments. The cement flamingos stand four feet tall in my back yard, and flamingos with spinning wings are in my vegetable garden. A dear friend made me a beautiful flamingo quilt.

Finding your own flamingos leads to the celebrating. I

believe my purpose in life is to help other people find their gifts—and a great place to start is by finding the gifts of your mother's life.

What are the gifts of your mother's life? This section is designed to share mine and help you find yours. Who knows? You may even end up dancing with your flamingos. Ready to cha-cha-cha? Or should I say, fla-fla-fla?

CHAPTER ONE

Optimism

"You live through the darkness
by what you learned in the light."
Hope MacDonald

"There's a silver lining in every cloud."
Mom

"Always look on the bright side."
Mom

Optimism is the perfect value with which to herald a new year and a new vision for your values. Optimism, the sense that there is a silver lining behind every dark storm cloud, gives us hope. Hope helps us look forward to better situations or times and not live our lives by looking behind us, wondering what happened, or harboring regrets.

Yes, we begin each New Year with a sense of optimism, ready to tackle the world with new-found energy and enthusiasm. My mom's optimism carried the family through long winters as we feasted on the food she had preserved the previous summer and delighted in the seed catalogs that promised gardening success the following summer.

SEED CATALOGS

Gardening on the prairie was an act of optimism. Hot days, strong winds and the ability to buy almost anything tempts one to abandon the hard work of digging, planting, weeding, and harvesting.

But then, the Gurney's seed catalogs came. When I was a child on the farm, they came every winter, offering us the dream of the taste of food fresh from Mom's garden. For a prairie kid, catalog pictures were an act of optimism needed in the middle of winter.

Of course, I wanted to order peas, my childhood favorite, because Mom let us pick, shuck and eat while standing in rows between the plants. Also my favorites were carrots, which tasted great, freshly pulled with a little dirt intact, and corn that I loved to husk. I loved almost everything Mom grew, and perusing the seed catalogs made me believe winter would end and planting time would begin.

What would have made it better? I would have liked to own and worn the green boots Gurney's included in the garden accessories. Bright green boots would have made gardening a bit more glamorous, and they would have kept my feet warm, and I would have looked cool.

Mom didn't buy them. She convinced me what my feet looked like in the garden would not affect the taste of green peas.

Spring always followed winter on the prairie and signaled that we were closer to the delicious fresh vegetables that Mom would serve. Today it would be called "organic gardening." Back then, it was called the way of life. Because it was so normal, I took it for granted.

Mom's gardening set an example I have followed my entire life. Moreover, I have actually taught those same practices to my grandson, Gavin.

GARDENING WITH GAVIN

"Grandmothers and roses are much the same.
Each are God's masterpieces with different names."
Author Unknown

At 7 a.m., the birds chirped and the sun shined, a welcome sight after days of rain. Tulips decorated my yard with splashy colors of red, yellow and white as I enjoyed my morning coffee. It's spring—time to grow gardens, plant flowers and enjoy every moment of the great outdoors in our own backyards.

Just before the five days of rain, my grandson, Gavin, and I decided to plant "our" garden, as he calls it. We selected seed packets of lettuce, carrots, beets, beans, cucumbers, flowers and a bag of onions. Recording the purchase in my checkbook, I realized it was May 3, Mom's birthday. I asked Gavin to guess whose birthday it was, and after telling him it was my mommy's birthday, I told him she was in heaven.

Mom worked hard in her garden, growing most of what we ate, and it was delicious. She was a great cook, meticulous in food preparation, clever in design, and superb with flavor. Thinking of Mom's green beans dressed with onions, bacon grease and vinegar still makes me drool.

As I worked in my garden with Gavin, I reflected on how hard Mom must have worked in her garden, which was at least 10 times the size of mine. If my back hurts, what did hers feel like? And just how many bug bites did she survive?

When Gavin and I planted our garden, I said that Grandma Betty loved to garden, and I was sure she would be our "garden guardian angel." We planted, sang our "Grow, grow, grow" prayer, and said "Amen!" while our garden guardian angel smiled down on us.

After five days of rain, we checked on the garden. Nothing had sprouted. We'd sing and check, sing and check. I started to get a little worried, looked up, and said, "Really Mom?" It then occurred to me that five days of rain had created a crust of soil that prevented the sprouts from showing. A little digging loosened the soil and up popped green bean sprouts. Gavin had his garden.

Yes, Mom, I'm telling Gavin about gardening with you…how much fun I had picking peas, how great raspberries tasted (especially when I knew I wasn't supposed to pick them), and of course, about your great torte created with rhubarb straight from the garden.

In my prairie child days, making rhubarb torte was an annual rite of spring. Picking rhubarb with Gavin just made it even better. And eating Rhubarb Torte was the perfect reminder of wonderful mom memories, just in time for Mother's Day. Remember and celebrate the happiest memories of your mom. If it's food, gardening or just enjoying a cup of coffee and conversation with another, use those memorable stories to comfort and share the values you learned from mom.

LOOK ON THE BRIGHT SIDE

Did your mom say, "Look on the bright side" when something went wrong in your life? Mine did. I didn't care much for that saying as a child, but now I cherish the value it represents: optimism.

Our moms taught us optimism in some interesting ways. For one thing, even though moms threaten to take our lives...justified by the fact they gave it to us in the first place...they never gave up on us.

Moms cannot give up on their kids. Like the needle of the compass always pointing to true north, moms have to believe their kids will always come through. We can always learn something new, achieve something better, or create something desperately needed.

Moms simply believed in us. Mine did. She always saw my bright side even when I couldn't see it. I'm sure she saw the other side as well, especially in my teenage years, but she played to my strengths as smart moms do.

THE VALUE OF YOUR OPTIMISM

Our values are gifts from our moms that become our strengths. In today's world, as with every generation, we need to be strong to face life's journey. The value of optimism is that it brings out the best in people. When we look at the bright side, we are seeing the best, and we always get more of what we see.

Isn't that a wonderful gift from our moms? That's one reason why it's so hard to lose her. She simply believed in us. She had to—she gave us life. That brought out the best in her, and in turn, she did her best to bring out the best in us.

Why not journal answers to the following questions to find your mom's gifts.

- How did your mom show you she believed in you?
- How did she teach you optimism?
- What did your mom say when things didn't go as you'd planned or hoped?
- Did she notice what you did right, and help you do more of it?

Think about your own level of optimism, and how your mom taught and reinforced it. I hope you find the same gift I found: a bright side in every situation, and even when I can't quite see it, I can trust it will eventually appear.

One of the real acts of optimism is getting married. But a close second? Shopping for the mother of the bride dress!

THE MOTHER OF THE BRIDE DRESS

"What I wanted most for my daughter was that she be able to soar confidently in her own sky, whatever that may be."
Helen Claes

For the second time in my life, I was about to be the MOB—mother of the bride—and that meant I needed a dress. That was stressful because I hate shopping.

Shopping is disguised torture. I tried on clothes that didn't look very good until I found clothes that did look good on me. Then, was I supposed to believe that the value of the item exceeded the cost, making it a great deal, regardless of the impact to my bank account?

I am cheap. Don't believe me? Just ask my daughter, the bride, whose stress over how I would look at her wedding resulted in the mother-daughter shopping trip.

I tried on every dress Kelsey brought me, and when I tired of every bulge showing and the appearances of bulges I didn't know I had, I was done. As we left the fitting room, I was surprised to see an aqua blue dress because I hadn't seen aqua fashions in a long time. I told my daughters it was the same color as our farmhouse that was destroyed by fire when I was 15.

Two days later, near the farm where I grew up, my sister delighted us with Mom's traditional Easter dessert, a family favorite called Calla Lilies. We talked about how Mom made the sweet dough and stuffed the Calla Lilies shapes with whipped cream. Mom loved to bake in her aqua farmhouse.

Then I shared with my sister about shopping for my MOB dress and seeing the aqua blue dress. Suddenly, she interrupted me, saying she had something I would really love.

MOM'S MOB DRESS

I did love Mom's mother of the bride dress from my wedding. The gown hung to floor length, had long sleeves and was aqua blue. I have few pictures of Mom and me, but the one I cherish is the wedding photo of me in my dress, Mom in her aqua blue dress, and Dad in a tux.

I married in 1976 when I was 20, young and in love. I didn't realize until after Mom died in 1990 that we were married and had kids at the exact same ages. Now I really like aqua blue, and to this day, I think of Mom every time I see it. We really do become our mothers, don't we?

Shopping for my mother of the bride dress reinforced the uniqueness of aqua. I rarely see a color that is emotional for me, but when I do, I instantly visualize my home on the prairie, amidst green lawns and brown fields framed by the endless South Dakota blue sky.

I know it was only a dress. But since I didn't have one yet, and the wedding was only a month away, I should I have told Kelsey I had fallen in love with the color aqua, and let her guess whether I had really become my mother after all.

Weddings are proof of an eternal optimism. We love, we marry, and begin a new life regardless of what dresses our mothers wear at our weddings.

- Do you remember the dress your mom wore to your wedding?
- Did you shop with her for her dress?
- Do you have a favorite photo of the two of you from your big day?
- Do you see smiles of optimism in those gathered to celebrate your big day?

BREAKING BREAD TOGETHER

The optimism of our mothers took on its own life in the kitchen. What else can be said for mixing yeast with water, adding flour and everything else the recipe calls for and watching it rise…knowing, trusting, believing that bread would be ready for a hungry family for dinner that night.

Mom was a great cook, a woman whose hands created and baked the sweetest, lightest dough to feed her family. I remember watching her bake bread, but never baking with her. Of course, after getting married, I wanted to bake bread like Mom had. That's when I learned it's a little more than yeast, water and flour mixed together.

Something called "kneading" was involved, with terms like "elasticity" which was followed by "doubling in size" which could be affected by "room temperature" and of course, "humidity."

Easily taken for granted, the taste and smell of homemade bread baking in the oven is the result of optimism in action by a mom who practiced, fine tuned a skill, and probably still smiles over my description of the first time I tried to bake bread like my mom. I'm sure we ate it....right Kim?

PRACTICING OPTIMISM

When I identified the values I learned from Mom, optimism wasn't at the top of the list. One day, though, I realized she encouraged me to find the good, even in the storm clouds, and to find the bright side in places that looked dark and confusing.

Now, optimism is at the top of my list because I believe few values change our lives with the power that optimism offers.

We desperately need optimism to offset the negativity that fills our airwaves and public conversations today. We're at war. The economy is coming out of recession. Loss piles up, weighing us down, unless we can find the hope in every day life.

Optimism helps us find solutions to real problems. Optimism brings out the best in us, and our commitment to live and practice it authentically eliminates our negativity. Seeing, even expecting the silver lining, makes our journey great.

The most fun I've had in becoming an optimistic person is the impact on my daughters. They seem to think I've become a bit naïve in my optimism. "Duh, Mom, there's nothing good about it!" Or, "You're just so cute, you and your optimism."

My mom said, "Practice makes perfect." Optimism is a both a gift and a skill I have cultivated with practice. You can too, and wouldn't it be fun to become so optimistic that we could bring out the best in people more often?

Choose optimism. It's a legacy that makes a real difference.

CHAPTER TWO

Compassion

*"Let no one ever come to you without leaving better and happier.
Be the living expression of God's kindness:
kindness in your face, kindness in your eyes, kindness in your smile."*
Mother Teresa

"A mother's heart is always with her children."
Proverbs

When I grew up on the farm, we had many cats. One cat in particular, "Mommy Cat," was usually pregnant. After yet another litter, she died. Mom saved every kitten in the litter by providing cow's milk—hand milked in those days—and using a medicine dropper to feed each kitten several times a day. They survived, and one we kept became a house cat we called Lucky.

Do compassion and luck go hand in hand? If we need help, we may feel lucky to get a break from someone with compassion.

Mom had loving energy for the underdog. Whether kittens without a mom, a baseball team, a horse in the Kentucky Derby—Mom cheered for the one deemed second rate and who wasn't supposed to win. My mother's hallmark was her cheering for the one not expected to succeed, the one not expected to survive, or the one who was down and out on their luck.

Mom backed her belief up with words, teaching me that compassion is an active word. When we say we have compassion, we do something about it: feed, donate, cheer and threaten the guy who insists upon cheering for the one predicted to win.

The source of a mother's compassion? Her heart.

A MOTHER'S HEART

Valentine's Day is about heart. When I was a child, I loved the heart shown at the end of the *I Love Lucy* show. Lucy was funny, but to me, she was also glamorous. She and my mom wore shirtwaist dresses, had beautiful hair, and wore shoes with skinny heels.

Mom had a heart-shaped brass mirror that was like a large locket. Pushing a little side button released the cover, exposing the mirror. I loved to play with it because it reminded me of *I Love Lucy*. When I opened the cover of the heart-shaped mirror, I could see myself in the mirror, and I felt all grown up, like a "big girl." I wanted to be like my mom.

When we look into our mother's hearts, we see love. Once when my daughters fought, obviously competing for my affection, I sat them at the old oak table for a lesson on a mother's love.

I told my daughters that a mother's love is the closest thing on this planet to God's love for us. A mother's love just is. You can't increase it; nor can you decrease it. It cannot be divided or multiplied. It just is.

Whether you give birth or adopt, a mother's love rises above pain, trauma and fear. Moms get a glimpse of heaven when they create life, and thankfully, God fills them with love for the tiny creature in their arms. That love only grows, not because of anything the child does, but because of the connection we have with God in bringing forth and nurturing lives.

I told my daughters, therefore, that I could not love one of them more than the other. I could not love them less, even when they drove me crazy. That kind of love is complete, whole, as perfect as life gets on this journey. Nothing they did could control my love for them. It just was.

My daughters' deer-in-the-headlights stares told me that they didn't understand my words, just like in another time when Kelsey was four years old. She and I were sitting in a friend's hot tub, and Kelsey naturally asked if we could get one. I told her we could, but her life would be much better if we saved our money for a college education and how much better her life would be if she went to college. Kelsey sat there pondering, and then asked, "So what's a college education?"

Moms want what's best for their children. Sometimes we just have to explain it.

My daughters did not understand the mini-lecture that day. That's okay. I didn't get the lesson either until I became a mom. Moreover, I understood the depth of the lesson when I lost my mom. That journey is the heart of the book *Dear Mom: Remembering, Celebrating, Healing.*

THE VALUE OF COMPASSION
Have you taken the journey of finding the gifts of your mother's life? Start with her heart. When you look in the mirror, think about the heart of the woman who raised you. Imagine her nurturing love that was always there, always supportive.

And then smile at yourself. You've become the best part of your mother—her heart. What a wonderful way to celebrate Mother's Day every day of the year!

> *"The best years of your life are the ones in which you decide your problems are your own. You do not blame them on your mother, the ecology, or the president. You realize that you control your own destiny."*
> Albert Ellis

VALENTINE'S DAY WITHOUT MOM
A mom's passing is a transition of remembering, celebrating, and healing with every memory, big or small. Usually small things we took for granted and now miss bring the smiles.

My friend faced her first Valentine's Day without her mom. I remember crying when I saw "Mom" cards for the first time after Mom's funeral. I sobbed as I realized with a chilling finality that I would never again send my mother a card telling her how much I loved her.

Moms give us so much…our very lives, our values, our senses of humor, tastes in food, our desires for plastic pink flamingoes. (Apologies to my daughters!) We took those gifts for granted. Much of our personal journey after moms die is about finding those gifts, holding them in our hearts, and claiming all the good.

My friend will miss her mom, even if death ended her mom's pain and suffering. Life without mom is a journey of transition that takes time.

If you're new to that journey, please take good care of yourself. If you have been on the "life without mom" journey for a number of years, reach out to those who are new to it. Listen as they remember the little things they cherish about their moms. We heal ourselves as we smile, recall the little things and celebrate the gift, the values you received.

And when you find yourself missing your mom, go ahead and tell her you love her anyway. I'll bet she's still listening.

PRACTICING COMPASSION

Practicing compassion helps us slow down in our busy lives in a media age where disasters and crises flash in real time across televisions, computer screens, iPhones and iPads. We risk becoming overwhelmed by feeling like we have no control, especially when our personal world runs a bit on the wild side at the same time.

Compassion focuses on others, a gift we give freely. This act of compassion actually returns our control to ourselves. We can control our own hearts to ensure we don't lose compassion in "heartless" situations. Remember the gentleness of the woman whose heart said baby kittens deserved a chance to live.

Let us practice the compassion our mothers taught anyway. Remember that we are all on this planet together experiencing the same stubbed toes, defeats in a hockey game or young persons being deployed to the Middle East. Only our ability to feel compassion—real, authentic compassion—keeps us connected and caring. That keeps our own emotional cups filled with blessings. Respond to these questions in your journal to help you reveal your mom's gifts.

- How was your mother compassionate? In words? In actions?
- Which compassionate act, the one that impressed you, do you remember from your mother?
- Was there a time when you expected your mother to be angry or stern when she became compassionate instead?
- Do you remember how you felt when she was kind to you?
- Do you practice compassion today? How is that a legacy from your mom?

Be compassionate. It's a wonderful way to make the journey great.

CHAPTER THREE

Kindness

"Kind words can be short and easy to speak,
but their echoes are truly endless."
Mother Theresa

"Treat others the way you would want to be treated."
Mom

If compassion is the thought and the belief of a mother's heart, kindness is the action that fulfills and delivers the heart's compassion.

Remember, no matter how mad we made our mothers, they could not kill us. Despite threats when we pushed to the edge and then some, they were still our mothers. And when they are gone, their acts of kindness—the unnumbered things they did with their hands—will live in our hearts forever.

A MOTHER'S HANDS

The gifts of our mother's hands were wonderful like the delectable cookies and treats and our favorite, homemade meals. It's easy to think of the clothes, both sewed and mended, or a home mom created for you, your siblings and your herd of friends.

There were also the less obvious gifts of a mother's hands: the touch that healed and soothed, consoled with a hot water bottle or a cold cloth. Let's not forget the almost instant healing bestowed by the magical Band-aid mom applied to all injuries, big and small.

I counted on Mom's healing touch when I was a child. Her long, lean hands were always available to me. Mom's hands were evidence of kindness, acts of compassion taught by doing what needed to be done to make life a little better, a little easier, for someone else.

JERGENS LOTION

One of my dear friends in Wyoming lost her mom. When I met her mother, I was so inspired by her amazing spirit that I wrote a *Dear Mom E-letter* in 2006 about her hands.

When I met her mom, I saw fingers that arthritis had cruelly tormented, had painfully and permanently turned inward. Her finger joints had dissolved, and the hands diminished to a small knot of flesh barely able to pick up food. These were the once strong hands of a ranch woman, my dear friend's mom, and were unlike any hands I had ever seen.

Her hands did not diminish her spirit that day I met her. Her energy soared, welcoming me, glad to meet her daughter's friend. She loved life and loved others unconditionally despite the severe arthritis.

A year after the funeral, I listened as my friend shared memories of her mother's hands. Despite being cruelly shaped by arthritis, her mother's hands were as soft as a baby's skin. How? With Jergens hand lotion.

I smiled and said, "My mom, too." I remembered my mom, dark hair curled, pulled back with bobby pins, wearing a shirtwaist dress, hands softened with Jergens lotion.

I could smell the clean, fresh, invigorating scent of Jergens lotion, and I smiled.

HANDS TAKEN FOR GRANTED

When you look at your hands, do you see the hands of your mother? Do you share the length of her fingers or the width of her palm? Do your nails resemble hers?

- What did her hands look like?
- Were they scarred and rough from a lifetime of work? Or smooth and silky?
- Can you remember her touch, her gentleness, and her care?
- Have your hands become the hands of your mother?

I took Mom's hands for granted. My friend's mother's arthritic hands reminded me to appreciate the hard work moms do without complaint. Moms bestow healing without need for our gratitude, and most certainly, they give love unconditionally.

If you're blessed to have the hands of your mother, tell her thanks.

MARCH MADNESS

Spring on the prairie was a busy time. Winter usually delivered one more unwanted storm before yielding to a colorful spring. Baby animals that were born in blizzards made farmers' lives more hectic. Also in March, in the midst of snowstorms and cows giving birth, just before spring officially arrives, I celebrated my birthday.

Mom made every birthday special with angel food cake with thick homemade Beat 'n Eat Frosting, colored pink, swirled to perfection. She rarely had the right number, but there were always candles. This was one simple, consistent act of kindness among many acts of kindness for which my mom was known, and I totally took for granted.

Soft, gentle, never a harsh word would be good descriptions of my mom. Other moms are a bit bolder.

- What was your mom like?
- Which of her words kindly encouraged you to offer your own acts of kindness?

PRACTICING KINDNESS

Moms teach us kindness through actions that demonstrate our compassion. My mom insisted upon kindness, regardless of whether or not I felt compassion.

We now know scientifically what our moms knew instinctively: acts of kindness make us feel better. Studies show that our acts of kindness create a rush of happy serotonin, a brain transmitter that makes us feel better, especially when we give someone else our kindness. Serotonin levels also rise when we receive that act of kindness. But the best news? They also rise when we simply see an act of kindness given to other people, and the more serotonin we feel, the longer our happiness lasts…all from an act of kindness.

- Did your mom teach you kindness?
- Did she model acts of kindness that made a very real difference for family, friends and neighbors?

Practicing kindness means being kind.

- What acts of kindness remind you of your mother?
- What acts of kindness do you practice because you were taught by a mom who cared enough to make a difference for others?

Mom said the world would be a better place if we all acted better. She was right, and the best action of all might be simple, authentic kindness.

Remembering Mom's kindness is a journey that makes me smile.

Practice kindness, a value you received. Others will be glad you shared.

CHAPTER FOUR

Resourcefulness

"Making the simple complicated is commonplace; making the complicated simple is creativity."
Charles Mingus

"Everything can be used again for something."
Mom

Mom kept life simple because she had a lot less stuff than those of us, the Baby Boomers, have accumulated. She lived on a farm or in a small town in a time of less media, fewer stores and no Internet. She had few spices, relied upon salt and pepper, and knew not the term "rub" for seasoning meat. The simplicity of her life was a model I sometimes miss.

Growing up, I didn't know we had little because we had plenty. We just didn't have a lot of stuff. Today I have a lot of stuff, and frequently wish I had less.

Is simplicity an important aspect to life today? Do we wish our lives were simpler? I do, but getting there seems to be like a long-distance marathon. I am more willing to wish for simplicity than to take action on it. Yet, every once in a while, I get an amazing reminder.

A JAR OF BUTTONS

Remember that time bomb called grief that explodes from within when triggered? Well, the one I'm about to describe began with a jar of buttons. A simple glass jar, sitting on a counter in an antique store, was filled with plastic and wooden buttons in varied sizes and colors.

Some people like my daughter might consider it a bit crazy to save all those mismatched, used buttons. She calls me a flea market decorator, and she may be right. I have old things, some wonderful, some simply sentimental, throughout my house. I'm frugal and sentimental, a dangerous combination for the person who loves flea markets and antique stores.

Seeing the buttons was an unexpected, comforting reminder of Mom. Then I saw green cups and saucers, red-rimmed enamel pans and coffee pots, embroidered dish towels and heavy white mixing bowls. I smiled and realized why I loved that kind of shopping. I felt really nice, like I was home in Mom's kitchen. Have you ever felt that way?

- Do you miss your mom's kitchen?
- Do you have your own "jar of buttons," something you save for use "some day?"
- Where do you go to find a comforting reminder of your mom?

Mom lived in a simpler time, had little, and saved everything. My brother and I described Mom as an early recycler. Nothing went to waste if it could be used again. Nothing. That included buttons. We never knew when we might need one or when we could match up enough odd buttons to use on a new blouse or dress.

- Do you save things your mother saved, just because?
- Do you have a jar of buttons in your closet or on your dresser?

It's just more proof that we really do become our mothers after all. Today I keep extra buttons in a small jewelry box. Have I ever opened it to get a button to sew onto a garment? No. Will I ever throw them away? I doubt it.

I have threatened to have a flea market bridal shower for my daughter. A glass jar filled with buttons would be a perfect gift! Or should I be more practical and throw them away? Of course not. I may need them someday.

When my granddaughter, named after my mom, visits, I miss Mom. I listen to her giggling, watch her play as she has learned to crawl, walk and run. I miss Mom at moments like that because I'd always assumed Mom would be there to see my children's children. And I'd hoped she would teach them to save buttons. But she's not. So the best I can do is make sure my granddaughter, Faith Elizabeth, knows the values of this woman whose life shaped mine, as I will help shape Faith's life.

I think I'll give my granddaughter a jar of buttons for her birthday in memory of her great-grandmother, the early recycler. And I think my daughter, Jess, will understand.

OLD CAT WOMAN

> *"Creativity involves breaking out of established patterns
> in order to look at things in a different way."*
> Edward de Bono

Creativity helps us find another use for everything. Being resourceful on the farm meant if you needed something, you made it from what you had on hand. Doing that required a creative approach that's still worth teaching today.

When Gavin was four, I had the chance to be with him for Halloween. I learned I would be working out West and could fly there in time to go trick or treating with him, and I called him with my exciting news.

I knew Gavin was going to be Batman and wanting to keep expectations low, I said, "Gavin, how would it be if Gumma would be Old Cat Woman?" ("Gumma" was Gavin's first—and thus far the only—name for me!) Thinking of my basic travel wardrobe, I said, "I have black shoes, black socks, a black top, a black leather jacket and black leather gloves!" Satisfied with my outfit, I was shocked when Gavin said, "Yeah, Gumma, and you need a tail!"

How would I make a tail? I shared that story with my dear friend, Mary, who grew up near Chicago. She said, "Now that's how you and I are so different. My first thought wouldn't be how do I make a tail, but rather where do I go to buy one?"

Quickly, I replied, "Oh, not me….with my mom, you didn't even think about going out to buy something like that. You

made what you needed from what you had on hand."
Of course, traveling and making tails are mutually exclusive
activities in a time-impoverished world. When I got to
Cheyenne…. voila! My daughter, Jess, had made a tail,
secured it with a large safety pin, and I went trick or treating
with my grandson.

And my mom smiled.

PRACTICING RESOURCEFULNESS

The blessing from living through hard economic times is
learning that we can make do with less. One way to do so is
to find another use for everything we already own.

Old denim jeans can be turned into rugs and quilts. Don't
throw them away. Give them to a non-profit to re-sell or to a
quilting group. I have decided that if stuff I no longer need
makes a difference for someone else, then giving it away is a
good use of my stuff.

As you remember how your mom practiced resourcefulness,
journal the answers to these questions to rediscover the gifts
of your mom's values.

- Did your mom teach you resourcefulness?
- Have you learned to "make do" with what you have
  instead of running to a store?
- Will you confess to washing Ziploc bags? (Please say
  it isn't just me….)
- Do you own more stuff than you need?

How much stuff do you own? If you were like me, the
answer would be "more than enough." Okay, then, what can
you do with it all? Recycling is a great answer to things that
you don't need.

Less is more in many ways, and that's a great value to share
with those you love.

CHAPTER FIVE

Simplicity

"Simplicity is the ultimate sophistication."
Leonardo da Vinci

"Do it right the first time."
Mom

In our hectic lifestyles today, how much time would we save if we did things right the first time?

Not a problem for you? Congratulations! For the rest of us, it's a great strategy and a wonderful goal for simplifying life.

I have friends who are wonderfully organized. I like them, but I am not like them. I know that when I focus and do things correctly the first time, it is a breath of fresh air. Saving time is a worthy goal in busy lives and one of the best reasons to strive for simplicity.

SIMPLE DELIGHTS

"Life is an amazing journey" has been the opening line of my inspirational presentations for a decade. I believe one of the biggest blessings we can acquire is the ability to balance the good and the bad so that we live in the place of joy, regardless of what the journey brings us. The simple delights make this possible.

I've learned some lessons that have helped me balance my life to make this journey the best ever.

First, I've learned to see beauty. Life is an amazing journey when simple scenes delight our souls. A thousand blades of grass topped with sparkling dew in the morning sunshine. Robins fighting over worms after the first rainfall in more than a month. Puffy clouds shaped like characters in Gavin and Faith's "Scooby Doo" cartoons. The bright moon, whether big, small, white or orange, is beauty in my eyes. I especially enjoy the full moon ringed with halos.

My life's motto is "Keep the pleasures of life simple." Doing this levels the playing field. No one can charge me for looking at the clouds, the moon, the birds or my grass. It's up to me to enjoy, love and then protect. Mom and Dad instilled in me a love for nature that continues to grow. The older I get, the more I value and become restored by nature.

Second, my secret has been to believe that good would always come from the bad. I learned this through the healing process of writing letters to a mother to whom I never said goodbye.

That healing was, and remains, the single hardest situation I've faced in my life. If I can find the good even in that journey, then I am free to find the good in everything. From someone who has walked that path, I invite you with my whole heart to free yourself of the "stuff" and find your balance.

- What are your lessons in balancing the good and the bad in life?
- Have you recently taken time to look at the moon, the clouds, a sunrise or a sunset?
- Have you arrived at the place where you find blessings in dark nights that were painful and despairing?
- If you could simplify your life, where would you start? Make your list now.

Keeping the pleasures of life simple makes the journey great. I hope you have the courage, wisdom and loving support from yourself and loved ones to see it that way every day.

SIMPLICITY OF THE SEASONS

I love the seasons. Living on the prairie ensures four distinct seasons per year.

Each season of the prairie is delivered with a beautiful simplicity that offers lessons we should take with us.

1. Spring always follows winter. Even after a dark spell, new life is just around the corner. Spring means baby animals—calves, lambs, fawns and ducklings. Spring brings

wild flowers, new grasses and trees full of blossoms that promise fruit by summer's end.

2. Fall always precedes winter. God gives us the beautiful colors of autumn, much like a quilt, to prepare for the cold, long days ahead. I believe it's His way of saying He'll keep us warm.

3. Summer produces what we plant in the spring: vegetables and flowers to delight both palette and eye. But if we don't do the work in the spring, we don't get the harvest of summer.

Mom died in the winter, a bleak time of year to lose someone. On the South Dakota winter prairie, grass is brown. Leaves are gone. Days are short. Logically I knew spring would come, but the first spring following Mom's death seemed a very far away.

As I look out at winter this year, I know spring will come. It might come roaring like a lion or sleeping like a lamb. But it will come. It always does on the prairie.

Just as spring always comes, so do the lessons of my mother. Like Mom, I am also a grandmother. I think of how Mom spent time with my daughters playing, helping them make craft items, and teaching them a few things in the kitchen.

Mom's time and effort richly blessed both of my daughters with a harvest of memories they still talk about today.

SPRING-CLEANING

Spring-cleaning was a ritual for my mom. She washed windows and walls, organized closets as she packed winter clothing and replaced them with summer shorts and tops. The last spring-cleaning chore every year was the worst: cleaning out the garage. It became a dusty, messy family affair, always proving the points that less would be more and that families can survive extreme cleaning.

The arrival of spring after a long winter makes me appreciate spring. Cleaning is connected to spring in many cultures. My friend, Elaine, researched the vernal equinox for a spring meditation she wrote and found evidence of spring-cleaning in ancient cultures around the globe.

I wonder if Mom had any inkling she was performing the same ritual as women did in ancient cultures. Or was she doing what her mother did, who of course, followed the pattern set by her mother, and her mother's mother.

Today, I am the spring cleaner. With great relief I cleaned out closets and drawers and even reduced the size of my library. With even greater joy, I cleaned the perennials and bushes in my front and back yards, making way for the new growth pushing up beneath the soil.

THE VALUE OF SIMPLICITY

Making way for new growth in us is the reason for internal spring-cleaning. That includes asking ourselves if we do things because someone else did them—like our moms—or because it's a good idea to do them.

Spring is a great time for us to emerge, to put on our personal new growth and create new habits. In spring, we review those optimistic resolutions of the New Year and re-incorporate the ones we are committed to manifesting in our lives, not only by doing more, but also by being more.

Spring is a time of hope, simplicity, and joy as plants and animals emerge from winter. Mom loved spring—from the first rhubarb and irises to the baby birds, goslings, fawns and calves. Spring is a time to celebrate and make simple our paths by clearing out what gets in the way. Make room for the new person emerging from within. It's a great way for us to become the best of our moms!

PRACTICING SIMPLICITY

As a child, I learned that money meant happiness. No one intentionally taught me that lesson. We didn't have much, and the people on television seemed to have more and that seemed to make them happy. I had to "un-learn" my illogical conclusion, verifying that a lifetime of simple pleasures adds up to treasures that make me incredibly rich.

Simplicity is an art form captured by painters, writers, quilters and chefs to communicate and share beauty. The essence of a beautiful thing is its simple design. Birds splashing water on wings in a birdbath. Leaves of grape vines showcasing a cascade of purple fruit.

All of that and much more in my backyard blesses me. The simple beauty beckons and holds my spirit and fills my cup, much like Mom's flower and vegetable gardens filled her cup.

Sadly, many in the world don't value simplicity. It can be deemed insufficient, lacking, or even a bit less than intelligent. I no longer buy into any of that. Simplicity is one of the toughest things to acquire, and its diligent pursuit is one of life's most worthy goals. Journal the answers to these questions to understand what deeper values your mom expressed.

- What simple tasks did you and your mom enjoy together? Taking walks? Baking cookies? Doing laundry? Gardening?
- What values did your mom's simple pleasures teach you?
- Is there one special story that represents the simple, enjoyable things of life you can share with your children or partner or friends?

I am blessed by my mother's value of simplicity, and I hope you are, too. We learn simplicity when we keep things simple, a wonderful value to practice every day.

CHAPTER SIX

Humor

"Laughter is the shortest distance between two people."
Victor Borge

*"Always leave the house wearing clean underwear
in case you are in a car accident."*
Mom

Humor and laughter open our hearts. Mom shared her value of humor all of my life. Life was not easy, but was always best lived with a bit of laughter, never directed at others, but shared to lighten their load.

Mom was funny. She had a unique, crisp sense of humor that made you laugh, usually because it reinforced a message. Remembering the gift of Mom's humor makes it easy for me to celebrate the fact that I have become my mother after all!

I'M SMILING BECAUSE I'M YOUR MOTHER

I found the perfect birthday card for my daughter. The cover read, "I'm smiling because I'm your mother." Inside, it said, "And I'm laughing because there's nothing you can do about it!" Was it a lifetime ago this little girl came into my world?

When I was about to become a mom, I feared I would die before my children would get to know me, so I wrote a journal for each daughter, beginning at birth. I wrote to them about everyday life, things they did and said, first steps and falls, lingering colds and toothaches. The record of their journeys depicted my love for them.

I copied 20 pages of Kelsey's journal—ages four to eight months—for her husband. He liked the idea of reading about his wife as a little girl, agreeing he needed all the help he could get as a new husband in understanding his wife. I decided to add copies of photos that matched the journal entries to make the story more complete, and that took me through the photo album of her first 12 months of life.

I saw evidence of how cute she was, how strong she was (she walked at eight months). She was a rascal, even then. However the photo of her big sister holding her and smiling proudly grabbed my maternal heart. Two daughters in Christmas dresses, four years apart, one adoring the other, hugs and smiles serving as evidence of a bond that can only delight a mother's heart—an image I never want to forget.

Like my own mother, I was 24 when I had my first child, Jessica, and 28 when I had Kelsey. Mom and I both captured Kodak moments, big and small, counting on film to remember things we never wanted to forget.

I cherish the black and white picture Mom took of my dad, my brother, and me bundled in parkas, poised on a sled that somehow held all three of us. I love her photo of me scowling as I faced the sun, wearing a dress I'm sure she sewed. And I treasure the Christmas photo of my brother, holding me, both of us smiling in front of the tree.

MEMORIES ON FILM AND IN THE HEART

Moms capture Kodak moments both on film and also in their hearts. Last night I felt the same pride and joy I'm sure Mom felt, looking back at a life she brought into the world and wondering where 24 years went. I smiled, knowing that the images and words that preserve the love of the first year of life are as much for me as they are for my daughters and their husbands.

How about you? Journal about your memories now.

- Do you have photos your mom took of your first few years of life?
- Do you have special Christmas photos that remind you of loving bonds with siblings that made your mom smile?
- Does your lifetime of memories encourage you to smile and remind your daughter that she can do nothing about the fact that she is, indeed, your daughter?

I called Kelsey and sang "Happy Birthday." Poor thing. She knows God only gave me the desire and enthusiasm to sing, not the voice. And she knows I easily forgot the two-hour time zone difference. But I was so proud of her when she politely thanked me, and then asked, very nicely, if she could go back to bed, declining my offer to sing another verse.

Kelsey knows I'm her mom. And I smile, knowing there's nothing she can do about it!

BALLOON HUMOR

I can't pop the pink, green, red and blue balloons that rest on the floor of the bathroom, bedroom and below the antique pew that borders the dining room. Each one reminds me of a little girl, her big brother and the absolute joy of this journey called life.

My grandchildren, then ages two and six, had just spent a week with us. Although Faith spoke few words, she was always busy, especially with balloons. One day at her home in Cheyenne, she discovered my briefcase supply of balloons (I was there for both work and play, and I make my seminars fun!) and when her little hands filled with color, I couldn't resist. I blew up dozens of balloons. Faith gathered them under the dining room table and sat in the middle of her collection, proudly smiling, triumphant in her gaggle of colored balls.

When we returned to Cheyenne for her brother's birthday in June, I again brought balloons. Faith found them and I blew up the entire bag's latex collection in designer colors of yellow, blue, green, pink and red. Faith again gathered them under the table and laughed joyously, sitting amidst her colorful collection.

HEARTS OPENED WITH HUMOR

Mom had many moments of humor as her granddaughters delivered simple joy by being kids—playing, making crafts, or reading stories. Take one granddaughter, add a pink balloon, pink cowboy boots and a plastic pink flamingo, and I'm sure she's laughing even now up above as she shares my joy and completely understands why I can't pop the balloons.

- Have you had magical moments recently with children and grandchildren?
- Have you laughed out loud at the humor they bring into your life with their smiles, their energy, and their love for something as simple as balloons?

I, too, have gathered some of Faith's balloons into a basket below the pew in my dining room. I look at the colors, and I smile. I feel her energy, see her smile, and think I'm the luckiest "Gumma" in the entire world to share such love.

These moments make the journey great. Don't miss them. Don't be too busy to blow up balloons, and don't be in too big of a hurry to pop them. Savor the joy, savor the love, and you will always enjoy the journey!

PRACTICING HUMOR

Balloons make most of us smile. So why don't we just buy a bag of balloons to have on hand? I do. I have balloons in every color I can find. I have used them for years in my workshops, but once I discovered how much fun I can have with Faith and balloons, well, there's always a supply on hand.

I recently watched an episode of *I Love Lucy* when I was working out at the fitness center. It was fun to watch black and white re-reruns of a show I enjoyed when I was a kid. Lucy's predictable forays into making every day life hilarious reminded me of the simple, healthy benefits of a good laugh.

It's good to laugh. Life can be hard, and humor can lighten our load.

- How do you remember your mother's sense of humor?
- Did she choose to laugh sometimes when instead she could have easily cried?

- In the healing journey of life after mom, tears and laughter mingle as we remember the joyful spirits of our moms. Is it okay for you to laugh and cry? Share such a story with me or a friend.

CHAPTER SEVEN

Patience

*"When you pray for patience, God gives you
a neighbor who throws garbage in your front yard."*
Author Unknown

*"Someday, your kids are going to do to you
exactly what you've done to me."*
Mom

When Mom said my kids would be like me, I think she was trying to teach me something, like I was a significant contribution to making her a very patient woman. Nice of Mom to give me so much credit!

- How important to you is the value of patience?
- When was the last time someone was impatient with you?
- How did it feel?
- How does it feel when you maintain patience with your grandchildren? With a neighbor?

Patience is a wonderful character trait to develop and practice, and it starts with lessons taught by our mothers.

ONE GRAPE AT A TIME

Patience is a challenge for my personality style. I've been called "Type Double A" by friends who know my "To Do" list never ends, and I feel guilty for not getting it all done. The next story reveals to you that perhaps there is benefit to a double Type A personality. I found it ironic that a little fruit called Concord Grapes would reinforce Mom's value of patience, one of the most important values in my life.

After moving to South Dakota, I purchased three grape vines to provide a natural screen to make my backyard more private and at the same time create a writing space. I selected Concord grapes only because I recognized the name.

In year one, the vines grew beautifully, producing a few clusters of green grapes that turned a deep purple. In year two, they produced even more. When people asked me if I was going to make something with them, I said Mom never made anything with grapes, so I assumed I didn't know how. I simply let the birds enjoy the harvest and washed the resulting purple bird poop off my chairs when I wanted to write.

Last summer, the grapes produced very abundantly. Purple clusters seemed to beg to be turned into something. So with plenty of practice making jam from our raspberries and strawberries, we decided to trust SURE-JELL and make grape jam.

Sometimes in life the problem is not the project, but the timing of the project. We began picking grapes at 5:30 p.m. one day when it occurred to us our daughter's arrival the next day would mean we'd never get it done if we waited. Purple clusters overfilled three large bowls, and what seemed like a good idea at the time ended at 3 a.m. We had enough grapes to make 27 jars of incredibly tasty, beautiful jam, each made one grape at a time.

One grape at a time. The trusted SURE-JELL recipe called for squeezing the skin off each grape. I could only find one way to do that—placing each grape between thumb and forefinger and squeezing to press out the pulp. We cooked the grape juice, and then blended the skins to a mush to add to the juice to get the purple color and perfect flavor.

One grape at a time. Every time my husband generously gives away another jar, I remind him to enjoy, because I will never make grape jam again. He smiles, saying next time we'll start in the morning instead of early evening.

One grape at a time. Like memories of childbirth that fade in recovery, memories of the amazing pain in my hands and back have been replaced with the pleasure of sharing grape jam with grateful grandkids and enjoying my favorite sandwich—peanut butter and homemade grape jam. As I share, though, I wonder how many jars of jam Mom made, one piece of fruit at a time, and how easily I took it all for granted.

THE VALUE OF PATIENCE

- Did your mom teach you patience the old-fashioned way?
- Did she model patience by working long hours on difficult projects?
- Can you remember her lessons, actions or words that encouraged perseverance, endurance and fortitude?

I'll bet she modeled patience silently, without complaining and by exhibiting a staying power that got the job done, regardless of hours involved, the summer heat or the piles of grapes she faced.

One grape at a time demanded a patience that drove me crazy, and believe me, I complained. (Sorry Mom!) But after the pain subsided and taste buds were delighted, the result was one of life's best gifts: the value of patience Mom modeled and tried to teach. Maybe I learned more than I thought I did. After all, I did it—one grape at a time.

PATIENCE WITH FAITH

On the first night of her three-week visit, Faith jumped from the chair to the ottoman to the floor. My heart leapt into my throat, and I frantically, urgently yelled, "Faith! Be careful!" She stopped, looked at me, and clearly enunciating each word, said, "I don't WANT to be careful!"

That sums up my granddaughter quite well. She is obviously determined to teach me patience, and you're about to understand why this isn't anything new!

CLIMBING HIGH

I was waiting to board a plane to California in September when I called my daughter Jessica to say I'd be in Cheyenne for her birthday on October 1st. I was shocked to hear she was on her way to the doctor with my then 18-month old granddaughter. Faith had climbed on to the top of her stroller, fell face first onto cement and was badly bruised. My daughter stood next to her when it happened, unable to respond in time to stop her.

- Have you been there?
- Have you been a mother when someone you gave birth to got hurt, when you were right there?
- Have you been a grandmother getting the news via telephone and wishing you were there?

Life is so precious, and yet it's filled with hard falls, the likely result of climbing so high when you're so little, even when your Mom stood next to you.

Moms stood beside us as we climbed all of our lives—onto chairs and tables, then up the tree, into kindergarten, through high school and beyond. Then our moms watched us climb and stretch into relationships, careers, and then, the ultimate climb—becoming moms ourselves.

Now we're the moms and the grandmothers, watching and knowing that climbing is natural, yet scared to death of breaks, bruises and concussions. We know our kids will climb and must. We know that little minds and bodies mature by tackling the physical and mental challenges life poses. After all, we gave birth to those limbs that need to see how high they can go. So we watch, nervously.

A MOTHER'S SAFETY NET
- What did your mom do when you climbed?
- Did she panic, warn, advise, beg, demand, predict loss of life and limb?
- Did she cave in and let you do what your headstrong character told her you were going to do anyway?
- Did your mom try to prepare a safety net for you like pillows and blankets when you were small, or practical advice when you were older?

- Was she always there to pick up the pieces and bandage the bruises?

In the tradition inspired by Germans and Norwegians of the South Dakota prairie, I raised two strong-willed daughters. I've seen them fall, and know my job is to patiently pick up the pieces. That has meant airplane trips, head massages and countless hours of listening to what happened when they climbed and fell.

This is an honor God bestows upon moms whose kids climb. We will do our part. We will encourage our kids to climb and stretch, just as our mothers did for us. And when they fall, we will be there. However, as I held Faith, whose bruises and concussion had healed, and whose brother is beginning to play hockey, I offer this practical advice, learned from my own mother: Encourage your kids not to tell you everything they're about to do. I can handle life better that way, can't you?

PRACTICING PATIENCE

Patience seems to be earned only the hard way in my life. Due to a back problem, I was stuck in bed at my daughter's house in Utah. I was supposed to be in Detroit, MI, speaking on *Dear Mom* to an international gathering of women. First Mother's Day for *Dear Mom*, and I'm in bed. I wasn't happy.

Gavin, then four, came up to me, patted me on the arm, and solemnly said, "Be patience, Gumma, be patience." Once again, out of the mouths of babes came the advice I needed to hear.

Being patient with ourselves isn't easy. Demanding, controlling, creating, fixing—all of those verbs are much easier to implement than being patient.

Be patient. It's a wonderful way to say you—and those you love—are worth it.

CHAPTER EIGHT

Cooperation

"We know one another's faults, virtues, catastrophes, mortifications, triumphs, rivalries, desires, and how long we can each hang by our hands to a bar. We have been banded together under pack codes and tribal laws."
Rose Macaulay

"Play nicely with your brother and sisters."
Mom

Was it helping Mom hang laundry on the clothesline? Was it learning to clean the house? Or was it mowing the yard, chasing cattle and doing whatever needed to be done on a farm that taught me cooperation?

Pitching in and helping, doing your share of the work was an early version of "teamwork" my mother taught. Isn't cooperation one of the values that makes a real difference in life?

CHURCH SOCIALS

We moved to a state park near my hometown when Jessica was two. At the time, I didn't want to live there. I liked my job in Sioux Falls and didn't really want to go some place I'd lived before. It didn't seem like a good career move for me.

I learned a lot by moving. We have lived in seven different communities in our married life. Each time meant getting to know people, learning about a new community and settling in. All of that is much easier if you have the value of cooperation.

Cooperation was a way of life on the farm. Neighbors worked together to harvest crops. Since it was expensive to own implements, farmers "shared" the burden by trading use of combines, planters and balers.

Cooperation when moving meant getting involved and working together with people to achieve common goals, like making homemade soup.

GERTIE'S SOUP

A small Lutheran church quickly embraced us when we moved to Lake City. That meant pitching in for the annual spring fund raiser, which was a Soup Supper. I had never made homemade soup. That didn't matter because Gertie told me how to do it. I complied. Then I brought my pot of soup to church, and was shocked when it was poured with all the other pots of soup into big roasters.

Convinced it would taste awful, I was instead shocked by the hearty flavor. The number of pies the church ladies had made surprised me, and more stunning was that we served nearly 400 people that day.

THE VALUE OF COOPERATION

I learned a lot about cooperation in Lake City. Making and serving Gertie's Soup was only my first lesson. Next came quilting, and those same wonderful church ladies were patient enough to teach me how to quilt by hand. Yes, stitch by stitch.

Years after Mom died, I still called Gertie for advice. Once she walked me through how to freeze chokecherry juice in milk cartons until I had enough for a batch of jelly. Another time she saw raspberries on my bushes. When she realized I had no idea how to make raspberry jelly, she made it for me. She even made it look easy!

Gertie taught me well. Living in Lake City was much like being on the farm. Everyone worked together, regardless of whether they always liked each other. They depended upon each other's support, kindness and help. And that's a great definition of the word cooperation, isn't it?

PRACTICING COOPERATION

Gertie was my mom's cousin and my dad's classmate. I was connected to her in several ways, including our work together in church where she was a matriarch, and I was a young mom.

- Who's your tribe?
- Who are your people?
- With whom do you love to work, play and build things? Bake meals? Frost cakes?

- How do you practice cooperation?
- How did your mom teach you cooperation?

Sometimes I fear our independence makes us islands. We can work alone, at home. We can work in cubicles on projects. Working together implies that not only is the end result important, but so is the process.

We learn from each other. We lean on each other. We grow, discover, and overcome challenges when we work together. And it's a nice way to live in the neighborhood!

CHAPTER NINE

Loyalty

"Lack of loyalty is one of the major causes of failure in every walk of life."
Napolean Hill

"If you can't say something nice about someone, don't say anything at all."
Mom

What feels better than having a loyal friend? Someone we can count on day or night? Someone who will answer our calls, listen and say things we know we need to hear? And when we forget what we need to know, they'll gladly repeat it without fuss?

Loyalty is easily seen in dogs. Our golden retriever, Charlie, was the epitome of loyal. With big brown eyes he listened, he consoled, and he tolerated my grandson's intrusively exploring nature. One day, two-year-old Gavin and Charlie stood side-by-side in my kitchen, heads at the same height, and Gavin had his finger up Charlie's nose. Charlie just looked at me, as if to say, "Now what do I do?"

We value loyalty. If we're lucky, we get to experience it with gratitude that fills our emotional cups with good stuff we can share with those we love on celebrations like the 4th of July.

4TH OF JULY

Mom loved America's birthday and picnics at Pickeral Lake where the quintessential celebration every July 4th was held. Of course, picnics meant food, and the 4th meant Mom's best: baked beans, potato salad, brownies—all homemade—with Kool-Aid and hot dogs. We had to wait an hour after eating to swim and couldn't wait for the water to cool us off.

Waiting to swim was not nearly as hard as waiting to shoot fireworks. My brother would entertain himself by throwing firecrackers at the outhouse when we were inside. Hearing the firecrackers, and need I say jumping for more than joy, prompted us to ask if it was time for fireworks. Mom and Dad replied the usual that we knew by heart, "When it's dark." We'd ask when the sun started to set, and hear, "When it's darker." We'd ask again and hear, "Pretty soon!"

We had to wait until it got really dark for the fireworks. Neighbors combined supplies, and we watched as our fathers and our older brothers shot Roman candles. Our "Oohs" and "Ahhs" led to our turn with sparklers, and we danced, twirled and created shapes in the air, all of which helped us forget about the outhouse events of the day.

The 4th of July is a celebration of freedom. Mom and Dad taught us that the best way in the world to celebrate freedom was by being loyal to America. This loyalty was not an option. Dad fought in WWII. My cousin was in Vietnam. We didn't always agree with what our government did or the wars we fought, but loyalty to America was unconditional.

Loyalty to Mom's cooking was perhaps even easier to develop than loyalty to America. Mom's cooking was the rave of many guests at many meals in my 34 years with her, and it earned loyalty because it was wonderfully delicious.

- What values do you hold dear about July 4th celebrations?
- Was there a specific tradition of celebrating freedom you cherish?
- How can you share that tradition with your family?

COMFORT FOOD—GRANDMA BETTY'S HOT DISH

There are many reasons why we miss—or will miss—our moms when they pass on. Their special ways with food, concocting a dish with simple ingredients, yet a full, rich flavor that smells a lot like love, becomes your family's favorite comfort food.

My mom's special dish was actually a hot dish, which is a Midwest term for casserole--a simple concoction of ground beef browned with onion, seasoned with salt and pepper, with vegetable soup and tomato sauce. Next she added elbow macaroni and cooked the noodles perfectly. We call ours "Grandma Betty's Hot Dish," and it's the first meal I cook after every road trip.

LOSING A LOYAL MOM

"Patriotism is just loyalty to friends, people, families."
Robert Santos

Another reason we miss—or will miss—our moms is one that snuck up on me and landed with an emotional "thump" that physically hurt.

I had traveled to Japan, Taiwan and Hong Kong with a group of other state travel representatives on a sales mission just weeks before Mom died. This was the biggest trip of my life. Once home I called Mom and did what I did every time I traveled: I told her about my trip, what I had done, what I had seen, what I had eaten and learned. She once said she didn't need to travel, because she traveled vicariously through me. (Yes, she actually used that word!)

Then Mom died suddenly.

Shortly thereafter, I flew to Denver for the mission's follow-up meeting. Then I had this choking feeling of deep sadness on the return flight home. I peered out the airplane window, looking at the black "nothing," unable to identify the sadness. Then it hit me. I had lost my safe place to brag. That would be the first trip of my entire life when I couldn't call Mom once I got home. I burst into tears, shaken, feeling very, very lonely.

THE VALUE OF LOYALTY

I could always call home and tell Mom about my trip, my latest adventure. It was a way of honoring her for raising me to be independent, educated, and employed in a great job. She gets the credit for much of what I am. My calling her was a way of my telling her that I was doing my best.

I can't call home any more. But I have replaced that phone

call with Grandma Betty's Hot Dish. This pure comfort food made in honor of Mom consoles me.

It's the first thing I make when my daughters come home, or when I visit them. Everyone has his or her own versions of Grandma Betty's Hot Dish.

- What's yours?
- Which of your mom's recipes or "hot dishes" makes you remember her caring ways?
- What do you cook for your children to convey to them that there truly is no place like home?

We can't buy Grandma Betty's Hot Dish. But we can cook it in love and enjoy it with our families while they tell you about their journeys, their lives, their dreams, their hopes, and their fears. We can smile as we become their safe place to brag, hoping they tell us more and more. Cherish the thought that this very moment is about as good as it gets, and we can hope for many more moments just like it.

THE PARADE OF SPARKLERS

I love to celebrate the 4th of July with my grandkids. We've attended parades and we've played in the parks. One year my daughter Jess made homemade baked beans. I made potato salad. We grilled some hot dogs, and patiently repeated many times to the grandkids the same phrase my mother used when we asked her "Is it time for fireworks?" "Pretty soon!"

My grandson knows my dad was an "island hopper" in WWII. He knows his uncle has served in three deployments in the Middle East. He understands loyalty matters—to family, friends, neighbors, community and country.

We teach what we know. Traditions like fireworks, picnics and parades give us time and places to remember something very special about America. Her birthday is July 4th; one we're blessed to celebrate every year.

When it was time, I watched as others—Jess, my son-in-law Aaron, Gavin and Faith—shot Roman candles, lit some snakes and a few firecrackers. When we were done, we retreated to the back yard and built a fire in the pit. With the last of the sparklers lit and in hand, Faith initiated a parade of sparklers…walking around the yard, smiling faces lit by the bright light. It was one more parade, one more celebration, and it made one more 4th July perfect.

COLORS OF SERVICE

Red, white and blue are more than the colors of our flag. They inspire in me a connection to service—military service, service to co-workers and customers, to family and friends.

We serve because we are loyal, committed to making a real difference. Loyalty shared with family, friends and community is part of what I believe we celebrate every 4th of July. Taking time to remember is a great way to give thanks.

Giving thanks is something I do very easily at my "church on the prairie." At least once every year, I go to Fron, a place that will forever hold my heart.

GOING TO FRON

I took my own unplanned, personal journey of remembering, celebrating and healing this last Memorial Day Weekend. I am renewed because of it.

Why unplanned? I thought I was just going to Fron Lutheran Church Cemetery to care for my family's burial place. I didn't realize I would sit on the graves and cry.

Sunday was a beautiful day. Clear, blue South Dakota sky, a gentle breeze blowing leaves and prairie grasses, birds singing and a cemetery bursting with color from peonies. My journey began by carrying water to family tombstones using what I had: a small plastic water bottle. Happy, twittering birds blessed three large granite tombstones identifying my loved ones last name, "HAUGE," with great frequency.

My journey progressed to scraping yellow and green lichen off the rough sides of the tombstones, washing away more bird poop, and making repeated trips to the water spigot with my plastic bottle.

Once washed and trimmed, I photographed the fern peony on Grandma Hauge's grave and sent the photos via e-mail to loved ones. Then I finished watering the peonies on Mom's and Dad's graves, having discovered an old, rusted metal coffee can that increased my efficiency dramatically.

When the work was done, my feelings surfaced. Unplanned and unexpected, hot tears streamed down as I stared at my parents' graves. But when I sat in front of the cross bearing Dad's name and honoring his military service, I bawled.

I miss my parents' insight, wisdom and humor that always let me know I would get through something. I miss having coffee with my dad, our tradition for nearly 14 years after Mom died. As I cried, I realized I had grief locked up inside that was clouding my vision, affecting my energy, and I wasn't even aware I was carrying grief around.

Mom and Dad never had all the answers, but they would always listen, and that helped me sort things out. Those "sorting life out" conversations were one-sided, but their ears listened and their hearts connected, and I always felt better because I knew they cared. On that day at the cemetery, I missed my Mom and Dad, and their hearts and their ears.

LIVING MY TRUTH

Memorial Day Weekend is a wonderful time to remember and celebrate the gifts of those we love and those we have loved and lost. For me, that includes remembering the values Mom taught, as well as Dad saying, "You know better," when I chose to not live the values I'd been taught.

I do know better, but I seem to forget. I seem to think that a bigger container always means I should carry more water. Isn't that life? I think I'm a big girl now, so I should be able to be tough and strong and carry more. After all, I'm a "Gumma!" and I have little people who look up to me, so I should be strong.

The older we get, the bigger our containers of grief become because the sheer number of people we lose grows. Yet we carry it, over and over, and then we wonder why we get tired, lose energy, and make some lousy judgments.

At least that's how it worked with me. And every once in a while, I "Go to Fron." I remember that my journey of healing began with writing a simple letter to my mom that released tears and pent-up emotions that became the book, *Dear Mom: Remembering, Celebrating, Healing.*

Now it is your turn to celebrate and remember your mom's gifts.

- Where do you go to feel safe?
- Where you can express grief, tears or pain?
- Is it time for you to write a letter now?
- Who will you write to and what will you say about the gift or value you are grateful for?

Some of you have had a year like mine. You've lost not one, not two, but three people in just a few months. Grief piles up, weighs us down, and we're not even aware of it. Find a way to release it. Find the place to go; find your Fron, and let the tears flow. I couldn't stop crying, but on the prairie, I felt pretty safe. And my wonderful husband hugged me, held me, once again supporting my journey.

Go to your Fron. Go someplace where you can write a letter, capture the essence of a memory, hold it in your hands, re-read it and know that the gifts of that person are as real today as they were when they walked this earth. They are simply in another place, still listening, still giving their perspective and gifts. That makes our cups overflow with memories that allow us to celebrate and heal.

PRACTICING LOYALTY

Loyalty to church, country, family and friends is something to never take lightly. People die every day for the freedom we enjoy. Loyalty helps us remember and celebrate all that's right about America and appreciate the people who raised us and taught us the values that will help us keep America strong. Appreciating that gift of freedom is the value Mom and Dad insisted we honor every year.

Teaching loyalty is a responsibility. I have several 50-ish aged clients who as leaders are concerned about the lack of loyalty they see displayed in the workplace by members of the Millennial Generation, a.k.a., Generation Y. My response has focused on one simple fact: Baby Boomers weren't hatched with loyalty. Someone taught us, and now it's our turn to teach others.

Loyalty is a wonderful legacy. As the world looks at us as beacons of hope, I hope our liberty bell rings on inside of us as we celebrate the gift of our freedom with Mom's potato salad.

CHAPTER TEN

Hospitality

"Hospitality should have no other nature than love."
Henrietta Mears

"We all ate a little less."
Bernice Zenanko

Golden Wheat dishes symbolized my mother's hospitality. Countless meals were served on beautiful cream-colored dishes with sprigs of golden wheat. I collected them after Mom died, and have collected sets for my siblings and my daughters.

The abundance of wheat dishes reminds me so much of Mom's ability to find one more seat and one more place setting. Somehow, some way, Mom always made room for more guests. As a child, I never caught on to how Mom stretched a meal. I never got a chance to ask her how she made a roast intended for us feed two or three more people. So I asked my other mother this question and learned a great deal.

MY OTHER MOTHER

My late aunt, Bernice, Dad's sister, was like a mom to me since Mom died in 1990. Bernice nearly quit school when kids made fun of her flour sack dress in the "roaring" 20s. I took Bernice to Norway the summer after Dad died. She's the one I loved to visit with over a cup of coffee and a cookie, much like I did with Dad while he was still alive.

Bernice grew up in the Depression. She was strong, in part, because she knew how to "make do," a phrase we used to describe getting by with less when you have to, an old technique now gaining popularity as we face rising costs of food, housing and energy.

- Do you have another mother—someone you trust, love and enjoy spending time with in person and on the telephone?
- What values does she model for you?
- What is the truest gift you gained from her and will pass to the next generation in your family?

I spoke at the new Davis Hospice Center, an incredible facility with staff members whose hearts offer compassion in a setting of tranquil beauty in Cheyenne, WY. I spoke on the concept in *Dear Mom* of how to find the gifts of a mother's life in her words, through her actions, and through metaphors like pink flamingos or Golden Wheat dishes.

One woman in the audience said she remembered how her mother always made room for another person at the table. Drop-ins were always offered food, a simple, sincere form of hospitality we offered to many on the farm. She posed this question though: How did her mom do it? How did our mothers always stretch a meal so there was enough for the unexpected? The memories made us laugh as we remembered and celebrated that story and the values of sharing and generosity.

Then I got a different take on it. Bernice and I were driving across the prairie we both call "Dakota." When I shared that story and the question of how moms did it, Bernice thoughtfully said, "We all ate a little less."

WE ATE A LITTLE LESS
Isn't that what moms really did? And I'll bet the one who decreased her portions the most would be the mom who prepared the meal in the first place. I' ve been blessed with a mom and other mothers—especially Bernice—who taught me the values of life that really matter.

- How did your mom teach you to share or be generous with what you had been given?
- Has it ever been hard to share with someone?

Sharing is a celebration—sharing food to feed, nurture and nourish is hospitality taught in biblical times as well as from those who taught us how to live.

I hope you take the time to remember, as well as celebrate the values hidden in stories you may have taken granted. It's a journey that heals and gives you the gift to pass on to the next generation.

My daughter will join us for a cup of coffee this morning. This other mother and grandmother, mom and daughter will share our stories that will strengthen us for this journey. Please remember to share your stories also.

A HARVEST OF HARD WORK

Summer means harvest on the prairie. Beans ripen in the garden, and fields of wheat, oats and barley turn golden brown, waiting to be harvested. We savored the fresh first ears of corn for dinner.

Mom's Golden Wheat dishes also reminded me that prairie life demanded hard work. My mom was an exemplary prairie woman because of her time and energy devoted to raising us on that prairie. The gift of her example is inspiration to get the job done…even when it meant another long day of baking food for her family.

BANANA BREAD LESSONS

Banana bread holds a special place in my family. Mom baked the perfect banana bread, and in her "waste nothing" approach to life, saved ripened bananas to use in her recipe. In fact, I wonder if you can even make legitimate banana bread using fresh bananas?

I have Mom's recipe in her handwriting that guides me every time I bake it. The recipe is covered in plastic, so I can drip egg whites on it without blurring her perfect handwriting.

EVEN CHARLIE

When we get to the end of life and look back, it could be measured in the number of loaves of banana bread baked.

Both of my daughters and husband love it, and even our golden retriever Charlie loved it.

One night when Charlie was still a "big puppy," I'd baked three loaves and had them cooling on the cupboard, which was an invitation to slice a piece, slather with butter and eat. Thus, the remaining two and a half loaves sat on the cupboard, cooling. When I returned to the kitchen, the banana bread was replaced by dog drool from one contented golden retriever too happy to even look guilty. Since that night, we could easily bribe Charlie with banana bread, the mere smell making him drool.

A DOUBLE BATCH OF BREAD

I don't bake often; but when I do, it is prompted by a freezer full of ripened, frozen bananas, and I need room to freeze something else. When I do bake, I'm usually in a hurry and I always make a double batch and freeze two loaves so I have something on hand for company. (Another "Mom" lesson!)

That night I baked the same recipe I've used for 20 years, making three pans from one double batch. Following Mom's perfect penmanship ("there's no excuse for sloppy writing") and her logical order of ingredients ("just follow the recipe, in order"), with the oven temperature memorized ("350 is the basic temperature for most baked goods"), and as always, I hastily turned the card over to read the baking time.

- Did you learn any special instructions for life in your mom's kitchen?
- Which of your mom's pies, breads or cakes were your favorites?
- What value does that special dessert bring to mind now?

INSTRUCTIONS FOR LIFE

In turning the recipe card over, I saw the instructions I'd

never seen or followed on the back of the card. The recipe was for a single batch, which I always doubled and put into three pans. But the recipe card said "two pans." No wonder I had trouble getting the middle of the loaf done. When I baked this double batch in four pans, it was perfect!

Our moms gave us the instructions we needed for life, but sometimes, the advice was hidden in places we took for granted or always looked at while rushing.

Slowing down long enough to find the values of your mother's life can be as simple as finding the value in baking banana bread.

HOSPITALITY ON THE PRAIRIE

Banana bread is about so much more than just great food. This comfort food extraordinaire, usually with a cup of coffee or a cold glass of milk, was a form of genuine hospitality on the prairie, passed from generation to generation. I have passed on this tradition from my mom to my daughters and to my grandkids, Gavin and Faith, who both like banana bread!

Next time you eat banana bread think of your mom, and guess how many loaves she made in her lifetime. How many loaves do you think she gave away? The value of hospitality is real, taught well by those hands and hearts that always had the ability to make another loaf of something good to eat. Their recipes fill my old wooden recipe box.

HOSPITALITY FROM THE PAST

There's "Lenore's Bread & Butter Pickles." Lenore was my Dad's sister who lived on a farm near Wadena, MN. Lenore's pickle recipe reminds me of the smells and activities of her kitchen. I spent many days during the summer learning that Lenore's methods of measuring were coffee cups and eating utensils, unlike Mom's standard measuring cups and teaspoons. Yet her food was beyond good. Her chicken would compete with the best anywhere.

There's "Pumpkin Harvest Bread" from my friend's mom, Louise, in whose kitchen I learned the joy of peanut butter on toast. She taught me how to create the wonderful blending of flavors in casseroles, a big change from the steak and potatoes diet we enjoyed on the cattle farm.

"Aunt Kate's Beet Pickles" is aptly named for my grandfather's sister, Aunt Kate, whose house I went to many Sundays after church. Her kitchen always smelled of freshly baked goods, and her porch was filled with plants, simulating a jungle in my child mind.

Some recipes have become well known by my daughters' friends. Kelsey has baked hundreds of "Kay's Caramel Rolls" for co-workers, fellow college athletes and for her husband. Jessica makes "Mom's Rhubarb Torte" for family gatherings, and both of them make "Grandmother's Chocolate Cake" for birthday celebrations, as I've done for 30 years.

There are recipes with names of my husband's family: LaVonne, Karleen, Grandma Edna, and Kay. There are recipes from my dad's sister Bernice. There are recipes identified with Norwegian names like Olga, my grandmother, in her never-changing handwriting, and I have a secret stash of several in my German Grandma Weyer's handwriting. Someday, I hope to frame a collection of them with my mother's banana bread recipe.

THE OLD WOODEN RECIPE BOX

Does your recipe box look and feel like mine? My recipe box looks like a disorganized, old wooden box filled with index cards whose corners are worn and bent. However, it is my treasure chest of loving memories of past family kitchens. It smells of family gatherings where your best dishes share your love, celebrate birthdays, or nurture and soothe a family after a death. Most of all, the spots and blurs on the recipe cards are like age spots on your hands, earned from a lifetime of service to those you love.

I love the recipes that were handwritten by the person who gave me the recipe. It's a very emotional journey when I look at penmanship I know I'll never see again, except for those precious, precious recipes, and I remember how each one who penned the recipe has blessed my life.

SHARING OUR GIFTS

One of my favorite "Mom" recipes is for her brownies. I featured it on my 2011 *Dear Mom Calendar* to the delight of readers who said it was simply wonderful. Those same brownies were the source of one of my best lessons on how sharing and hospitality are closely related.

One day my mom's pan of brownies was reduced to one brownie. I held the knife, prepared to cut the brownie into two pieces to share with my sister. Either the placement of the knife or the look in my eye gave Mom a clue as to my intentions. Knowingly, she said, "You get to cut the brownie in two, but your sister gets first choice of pieces."

Isn't life like that? Sharing fairly brings the spirit of hospitality to action. And it's evidence of other gifts, including trusting God there will be more, and faith in knowing that it's always the right time to do what's right. We celebrate and give thanks by sharing what has been given to us.

One of the first television interviews I had after publishing *Dear Mom* was with Doug Lund, long-time journalist with KELO-TV in South Dakota. It was the first time a reporter asked me why I wrote *Dear Mom*. Without hesitation, I said, "Have you ever received a gift that was so wonderful, the only way you could give thanks was to share it with others? That's how I felt about the healing I got from writing letters to Mom. I healed from incredible pain. I wanted to share that gift with others."

PRACTICING HOSPITALITY

I miss the era when people arrived unannounced just to see you, say "Hi" and catch up on life. Once Mom's aunt from Helena arrived on the farm unannounced. She walked up to our doorstep, heard Mom yelling at one of us, and shouted to her husband who was still in the car, "We've got the right place, Marcus!"

We've got the right attitude, I believe, when we open that door and share a cup of coffee, a cookie, or a piece of banana bread. We've got an even better attitude when we invite our guests to stay and turn dinner for four into the hospitality for a few more.

I learned a huge lesson from Bernice when she said, "We all ate a little less." Sometimes we do. Isn't that what hospitality is really all about? Sharing what we have is a way of giving thanks, and that value makes the journey great every day.

CHAPTER ELEVEN

Quality

"Apply yourself. Get all the education you can, but then, by God, do something. Don't just stand there, make it happen."
Lee Iacocca

"If you're going to bother to do something, do it well."
Mom

I can at any time, in any place, hear my mother's voice say, "If you're going to bother to do something, do it well." I hated hearing that when I was dusting the floors in a hurry or trying to get by with other chores. But it became a mantra, a belief, that life isn't just about what we do, but how we do it. The "how" says a great deal about us.

ME, TOO, MOM!

I'm the sort of person who tries Netflix not for current movies, but for the old ones I've always wanted to see. One of my goals is to watch Katherine Hepburn's early movies. I love her as an actress, and I also enjoyed her colorful writing style, which she shared in her autobiography titled *Me*. Shortly after she wrote her autobiography, Snoopy from the Peanuts comic strip was on top of his doghouse writing his autobiography. The title for Snoopy's? "Me, too."

I call it the "Me, too," factor. When we see something really good, we are naturally inclined and inspired to replicate it in our own lives.

That's why it can hurt so much to lose your mom. We wanted to be like her. We wanted to wear her lipstick, her necklaces and bracelets. We grew up wanting to cook her special food and bake her favorite cookies. We even wanted to make her favorite preserves and pickles. I made Mom's Bread and Butter Pickles by hand, something I've never done before. I have shared in presentations how Mom made gallons of those pickles by hand because there were no food processors in those days. Mom just had an old butcher knife, sharpened by hand and used to cut hundreds of cucumbers into thin slices.

I've used my food processor for cucumbers in the past, but got too many goofy-looking slices. When my garden surprised me with several gallons of cucumbers, I figured they deserved the justice of being sliced by hand so they would be beautiful, just like Mom's.

PRESENT MOMENT, GRATEFUL MOMENT

As I sliced, I relaxed. I remembered Mom growing, picking, slicing, and preparing the food that fed a family on the prairie, and I smiled. I stayed in the present moment and focused on my "To Be" list, instead or worrying about all the items on my "To Do" list. I sliced over and over those beautiful cucumbers that grew in my garden, and I gave thanks for the harvest and for the quality of food that I take for granted. In fact, I expected to be able to produce for my own family, just like Mom did for hers.

The irony of this little adventure was that as a kid I didn't even like Bread and Butter Pickles. I had no appreciation for the many jars that sat on the wooden shelves in the basement. I preferred the jars of canned cherries, canned crab apples-- complete with stem, as well as all the jars sealed with wax to preserve chokecherry and plum jam.

My love for Bread and Butter Pickles was an acquired taste, now the perfect topping on Grandma Betty's Hot Dish, my replica of Mom's goulash that has been my family's soul food.

The results of my desire to be like Mom? Fifteen pints of Bread and Butter Pickles in my pantry. I opened one yesterday to dress up a chicken salad sandwich. I darn near drooled over the flavor. The irony? I chopped the pickles before mixing them into the chicken salad, so their appearance didn't matter. But they sure looked beautiful in the jar!

The "Me too," factor is strong, like a magnet that pulls us toward things we want to be or do or have in our lives. I garden like Mom gardened because I love the food she prepared, and if I don't make it, I don't eat it. One cannot buy my mom's pickles. One can only make them. I cannot buy my mom's Blue Plum Pie. I can only make it, which I did recently for my brother so we could share a bit of Mom.

WHAT'S YOUR "ME TOO" FACTOR?

- Where in your life have you said, "Me, too," as it relates to your mom?
- What do you create, make, bake, cook or do because your mom did?
- What kind of values did her cooking and creating efforts gift you?
- What things do you make, just so you can share a bit of your mom with your family?

The biggest example of my mother's life wasn't her pickles, as good as they were. Quality, hard work and kindness were her way of saying, "I love you." It wasn't easy to raise a family on the prairie without a food processor. But she did it, and she did it well.

When I told a friend in Michigan how I made pickles from cucumbers I grew in my garden, she said, "You really are a prairie woman!" I smiled, taking it as a huge compliment. Then I looked up, my way of seeing Mom, and said, "Thanks Mom. Me, too!"

PRACTICING QUALITY

Mom simply and effectively set the bar high for quality. I was raised to believe that my job was to do the best I could. In fact, Mom said, "A little hard work never hurt anybody," and "Practice makes perfect." Sound familiar? Echoes from your past also?

For a while, Mom's phrases made me think I had to be perfect. I still struggle with that concept, but it has been largely replaced with this: I can always do my best and be my best in the moment. That is now how I define perfection. Some days truly are better than others. To know that my work matters, that I am on purpose with my life, instills in me a desire to have the stamp of quality go into whatever I do.

Now I just wish I used that philosophy when I cleaned the bathroom. Oh well…so much for perfection!

- What does "giving it your best effort," mean in your life?
- Do you apply it to your career, your home, and your closets?

Quality is one of those overriding values, which connects all other values. We know quality when we see it. We know it when we do it, and when we don't do it. As Dad said, "You know better," when I chose not to do my best.

I believe we all know better, and our knowing better can inspire us to be better.

CHAPTER TWELVE

Creativity

"But out of limitations comes creativity."
Debbie Allen

"Everything can be used again for something."
Mom

In my mother's world, everything could be used again for something. Bread wrappers were cut into long, thin strips and crocheted into rugs that caught a lot of dirt on the farm. Old jeans were cut into 1" by 6" strips and sewed into a rug that caught even more dirt and gravel. And the ultimate? Even Dad's big old used-to-be-white underwear could be turned into dusting cloths. Geez, Mom!

Today's economic struggles mean this value is incredibly important. But shouldn't we always stress reusing, recycling and finding a new use for something? Being "green" should be more than a trendy belief used to attract people to buy certain products. "Green" should be a way of life, and if you had my mom, it would be. Of course, there's a real downside.

LIFE AS A PACK RAT

Raised to believe that everything can be used again for something is my best excuse for being disorganized. When everything can be used again for something, you can't throw it out. You must keep it. But where? Boxes. Bins. Closets. Don't even mention the garage because I married a man whose garage holds evidence that many things can be reused in another time for something. At least he's organized in his collection of stuff!

Pack rats beware! Those naughty rats breed disorganization among us!

IT'S ALWAYS SOMETHING

Gilda Radner and Mom shared a simple philosophy: It's always something.

Today I proved it. Inspired to write, I dressed and proceeded to the bathroom to brush my teeth. Seeing proof that yesterday I had planned to clean the bathroom but didn't complete the task reminded me it was time. So I stopped, cleaned, returned to my computer several times to complete a thought that had seemed like a good idea earlier in the morning, but typing wearing yellow gloves was challenging.

Returning a glass to its rightful place in my kitchen instead of my bathroom reminded me that I needed to eat, something that occurs to me usually about mid-morning on my "writing" days. So I ate...which reminded me that my kitchen still smelled bad from last night's good idea to not cook. Rather, we relied on Papa Murphy's Pizza that we bought and baked at home.

The fire that erupted in the oven last night reminded me that I hadn't cleaned the oven since I'd had the bright idea of baking six squashes for freezing. Each squash left a deposit on my oven floor, and when combined with 425-degree heat, became a bright, raging fire that destroyed the heating element. My husband was out purchasing a new heating element, and I had an oven mess to clean up.

REALISTIC EXPECTATIONS

Isn't it always something? Mom seemed to know this in a way that nicely reduced her expectations. She didn't think she could do it all in one day, or even in one week. So why do I think that I can? I just know that every time I multitask, and I return to my computer wearing yellow gloves, I'm in trouble.

It does seem to always be something. For me, it's the quick tasks. Like, "If I go fast, the bathroom will be cleaned in five minutes!" Yes, it's possible, but not likely, especially given the fact that whoever built this house had the demented mind to put white tile around a white tub along with white cabinets.

Do you know how often white looks clean? And do you know how dirty white really gets? Yuck.

Which leads me back to my oven logic, thinking, "Five minutes? No way. Okay, ten!" Hours later, it's done. Almost. There is, of course, an easier solution. I can see your brain cells working now. You're thinking, "Duh, Dee Dee, don't you have a self-cleaning oven? Or a housekeeper?"

Yes, and no. Yes, I have a self-cleaning oven, but my kitchen has those same white cabinets as my bathroom, and the last time I asked the oven to clean itself, it melted some of the finish off my cabinets.

No, I do not have a housekeeper. Friends who had the guts to come over for dinner suggested that I get a housekeeper. Should I take the hint? Especially since they haven't returned recently?

My mother knew it was always something. She also knew it wasn't a good idea to have white cabinets. Maybe I should add a new kitchen to my "To Do" list?

The last time I did that, my mother died suddenly while my kitchen was down to bare walls. We were using our bedroom as a makeshift kitchen, and the new cupboards in large boxes filled the living room. Yes, 20 years ago this December, my house was in chaos. So no, I won't even think about new cabinets.

I've healed more from my mother's death than from the upheaval of the remodeled kitchen. I'll just let Comet help, and the next time I wear yellow gloves back to my keyboard, I'll smile and know it really was something.

THE GIFT OF A SISTER
The friendly waitress asked if we were sisters. Surprised by the question, I replied, "No, but I'd be honored if we were!"

The waitress went on to say how couples begin to look alike with age, how friends like us begin to look alike, and how people and even their pets begin to look alike over time. I understood and smiled, thinking of side-by-side photos I'd seen of people and their pets with similar hair, mustaches and even grins.

But have my friend and I begun to look alike? We've shared intimately the details of life without my mom. My friend was one of the first to read my book, which came out shortly after the death of her own mother. We've shared details of our careers—the successes and overwhelming minutiae that attack women who try to do too much, but then do it anyway. We've shared the joys and challenges of raising children—two moms struggling to be as wise as we are loving.

My friend is a quilter. It's her art, her creativity, and her passion. She quilts using old fabric and new, on an old Singer sewing machine—the exact model Mom used to sew my clothes. Nearly everything I wore—blouses, dresses, skirts, coats, shorts, pants and tank tops—all came from Mom's hands guiding fabric under the black body of the old Singer sewing machine.

Just like the values of my mom, the old Singer wasn't very complicated. Stitches could be straight or zigzag, long or short. It didn't require much maintenance, just a little oil stored in an old tin can. That was about it. The old Singer was simple, dependable, and strong.

My friend used her old Singer and some of her grandmother's fabric to create a pink flamingo quilt for me for my birthday. It's a *Dear Mom* quilt, which was stitched and shared in love. Being crafted on the Singer reminded me of Mom, and how we do become our mothers, inside and out.

- Do you create the same things your mom created?
- Do you have things she made, and do you find them priceless?
- Do you have a friend with whom you've shared the intimate journey of life and now you've begun to look like her?

Losing your mom is one of the hardest journeys of your life. Don't travel it alone. Share your memories over coffee. Share your cherished traditions over lunch. And when a waitress asks if you and your friend are sisters, just smile and enjoy the honor of being lucky enough to have such a great friend.

PRACTICING CREATIVITY

Mom's creativity inspired an effective form of problem solving, especially when combined with the value of optimism.

First, you simply have to believe you will find a solution to whatever challenge you face. Claim and believe that. Then, you have to look at things from different angles.

"Everything can be used again for something" strongly suggests multiple effects available without changing the core, and that can change the outcome.

When you need to fix, improve, change something, thinking creatively is one of the most affordable, team building, attitude-changing actions you can take.

All of that from a mom whose creativity was both natural and reinforced by need. It's a great combination we can all use to make our world a better place.

CHAPTER THIRTEEN

Beauty

*"The only difference between the beauty of one person
and the beauty of another is
the concept of beauty that people have."*
Don Miguel Ruiz

"Gumma, I just love your pink flamingos!"
Faith

What's your concept of beauty? Is it physical—taut muscles, natural body weight, or thick hair? Is it mental and emotional—a positive attitude, a kind spirit, or a gentle heart?

Beauty is all around us. Soaking up the sunshine, sitting outdoors amidst a blooming garden, and being at one with nature are all steps I take to absorb the natural beauty of everyday life. I walk. I sit. I play in my yard, absorbing nature's colors, sounds, and fragrances.

What about the beauty of people? My efforts to forgive, love, take the best and leave the rest are all related to beauty. I will look at the good—the beautiful part of a person—and build upon that in our relationship.

Beauty relates to purpose. A beautiful person is the one who glows despite sweating because she is on purpose. She knows why she's here on this journey, and she embraces that purpose with enthusiasm and determination. That kind of beauty is energy unleashed and used for a greater good—serving God and His people.

The beautiful person with clear purpose stands tall. Her shoulders are back. Her voice is clear. She knows, serves, creates, and acts with radiant passion whose glow invites others to share the journey called life. She offers her beauty with no strings, only love, which makes her offer enticing.

Beauty is irresistible. We are drawn to it and energized by it. Beauty is harmony, cooperation, and intuition. Beauty is looking for and finding the best in a person, no matter how buried or disguised. Beauty is gentleness, patience and kindness—practiced with those who are not.

Beauty is a gift that each of us received from our moms.

That doesn't mean moms are perfect. I am the first to hold

up a mirror and see flaws. Flawed, flogged—mostly by myself for being flawed. Women expect perfection, demand incredible results and keep impossible schedules. And that's just on Monday.

Letting go of expecting perfection from ourselves is a great step in letting go of expecting perfection from others, including our moms.

- How do you find beauty in people? Do you hear their words? Feel their energy?
- What was your mom's beauty – in her physical form, emotional strength, ideas, and actions?
- Will you create something beautiful today?
- Will you share a story of beauty with a friend or family member to help you stay positive and upbeat?

"When we know better, we do better."
Maya Angelou

Like us, our moms had too much to do, but did the best they could in the situation they were in with what they had at the time. Truly knowing that our moms did the best they could allows us to release the emotional stuff we no longer need, and replace it with affirming the good, the blessings, the values.

The beauty in each of us is no accident. We're here by design. God created us, flawed we became in the process of growing and maturing, learning and living and loving. I think scars, birthmarks and wrinkles are beautiful—proof of life born, lived and survived. That alone makes us objects of beauty.

WHAT'S IN YOUR GARDEN?

Mom expressed beauty in many ways, and my favorites were her flowers. From tall hollyhocks to short petunias, from perennial peonies to seasonal geraniums, Mom's garden of floral delight seemed easy since I wasn't doing the work. That made it easy to take for granted.

Daisies were one of Mom's favorites. Not the large, strong shasta daisy, but the smaller flowers with two-inch wide blossoms. I call them "happy flowers" that "smile" in my prairie yard.

Flowers are like people. Just as we select flowers for our garden, we select people who we take with us on our journey. We choose a variety, based upon characteristics that make us smile, remind us of different paths in our lives, and help us be the best we can be.

My heritage garden has flowers from Mom, aunts and friends who have shared their floral and personal beauty with me. Of course, the heritage garden is also home to those pink creatures that remind me of Mom's legacy of values. Moreover, my pink flamingos seem perfectly content to call my garden home.

PRACTICING BEAUTY

I think seeing the best in people is the closest we come to being angels while we're here on earth. We easily see the flaws, especially when we've been hurt. To see the good in people—to see the beauty of a person's spirit—despite what we're dealing with, is to discover the spiritual part of a person, sometimes hidden quite well, but nonetheless there.

I believe it's our job to see the best in people. I don't wear a halo, and I don't do this perfectly. However, my goal is to see the beauty around me, in myself, and in others.

There's a lot of beauty in the world. Far more than my eye can see.

CHAPTER FOURTEEN

Gratitude

*"When I'm weary and I can't sleep,
I count my blessings instead of sheep.
I fall asleep counting my blessings.
When my bankroll is getting small,
I think of when I had none at all.
I fall asleep counting my blessings."*
Irving Berlin

"Count your blessings."
Mom

Within days of the 20th anniversary of my mother's death, I saw the movie *White Christmas* for the first time. I'm surprised I had never seen it, especially since Mom and Dad loved Bing Crosby. I remember the classic *White Christmas* as a song, but not a movie.

Now I know the source of the phrase that became popular before I was born and shaped my life. The song, *Count Your Blessings,* was featured in that movie. Hearing it reminded me of the simple, sincere, spiritual principle Mom taught with those same three words: "Count your blessings."

HARD MOMENTS

Saying goodbye in October to the man who married your daughter in May is one of life's hard moments, especially when he is deploying to Iraq.

Three days after saying goodbye to Dave, I was back home, and I woke up in a funk. I didn't like my house because dust accumulated when I'm wasn't there. I didn't like the leaves filling the backyard despite the fact that autumn is my favorite season.

As I wrote in my journal, I wondered what I would tell members of an audience to do if they woke in a funk. Immediately, I heard my mother's voice say, "Count your blessings."

I looked at my furniture and gave thanks…despite the dust. I looked outside and saw the beautiful colors of maple, aspen and apricot leaves instead of the work their presence on my lawn implied, and I gave thanks.

Then I thought, "And Dave is still alive." I gave more thanks. I counted my blessings. Now I count my blessings every morning, and when I remember, count them also at night.

- What was your mom grateful for in her life?
- What are you grateful for right now?
- Why not take a moment and tell someone you love how much you appreciate him or her today?

Someone else will always have more than I have. I will always face loss. Things can always go wrong. But if I remember to look at the sky and see the gift of God's creative color palette in another perfect South Dakota sunset, if I can listen to the flock of geese and hear the swoosh of their wings just yards above my head, if I can think of all the joy I have right now, in this day, in this moment, and I can give thanks, I have just changed my life.

Another way Mom taught gratitude was Thanksgiving dinner. Being the great cook she was, I cherished our holiday dinners my entire life.

THANKSGIVING WITHOUT MOM

Thanksgiving without mom is noticing the one missing around your table as the family gathers. Noticing is lonely. Holiday grieving is especially painful, whether you lost your mom recently or long ago. Those mom memories, imprinted in our hearts and souls, rise up for notice during the holidays.

Each of us may know a close friend or relative who has lost her mom because there are nearly 40 million Baby Boomer women connected to their moms in this country. Losing mom means losing the one who spent thousands of hours raising us and working hard to create the Thanksgiving traditions we cherish.

Remember how our moms prepared for Thanksgiving—selecting and roasting a turkey, planning a menu, baking the pies the day before, finding delicious stuffing recipes. Then…voila! The sumptuous, festive dinner graced your table. Did some of us take it for granted? I did, and the memory of Mom's Thanksgiving feasts still makes my mouth water. My favorite Thanksgiving memory is watching parades on television while smelling the banquet delights.

Mom was quite traditional in her menu.
- Turkey, roasted to perfection
- Dressing (I didn't eat it)
- Corn Mom had grown and frozen
- Yams (yuck!)
- Buns (made from scratch)
- Lefse (the German succumbed to making this Norwegian potato flat bread for her Norwegian husband and kids), and
- Cranberries in relish I never tried. It looked way too adult for me. (Sorry Mom!)

The best dishes of the feast were her famous pies. One letter in *Dear Mom: Remembering, Celebrating, Healing,* describes Mom's perfect crust. Mom trimmed each pie crust by gripping dough between thumb and index finger. Then she twisted delicately to form the perfectly spaced edging. She made cherry pies—my favorite—and I could eat half of one pie at a sitting, earning my nickname of Hollow Leg.

IMPRINTED MEMORIES
- What Thanksgiving memories have imprinted on your heart and soul?
- Is it mom's main course or delicious desserts?
- Was it having cousins and relatives to play with?
- Who joined you for dinner?
- Did your mom use her best dishes or fine silver?
- Did your mom make fruit pies like mine did?
- Write your favorite Thanksgiving story and share your memories with someone you love.

Each of us likely knows someone who is facing her first holiday season without mom. Perhaps it is your first

Thanksgiving without mom. That means mom is missing from the table. Her chair is empty. Worse yet, she's not cooking any of the favorite foods. The feasts we've always known are changing.

Grieving at this time of year is especially hard. The rest of the world continues with music and parades while some of us miss our moms. Counting the blessings from our mothers' lives is a great way to heal.

COUNTING MY BLESSINGS

I have an annual tradition to "count my blessings" at the end of the year. Gratitude is reverent payment for gifts we receive, many of which were free, therefore, easily taken for granted. At the end of the year, I'm rich after noting my blessings. What the dollar amount is in any account doesn't matter. I am rich with blessings.

I know the joy of my granddaughter's toothless grin while opening presents with her brother on her first Christmas. I love sharing with my grandson the glow of moonlight on freshly fallen snow, and the colors that burst profusely from a sunset, and then quietly disappear into the dark of a starlit night.

Over the past five years, I have been blessed to have a file filled with cards, letters and e-mails from people who have read *Dear Mom* and let me know the joy it gave them.

I am so grateful for you!

You are one of my blessings. You have shared the journey called *Dear Mom*. You've shared memories of your own mother's hands, her food and holiday traditions. One of you even shared a cookbook filled with mom recipes and stories that described the making and sharing of food and memories surrounding those wonderful meals.

You've shared stories of losing your mom and stories about your mom with dementia. You've shared stories of love and lessons learned. You've shared the journey in a way that honors your mom, the fact that we all become our moms, and the legacy we're going to pass on now that we are moms and grandmothers.

Ours are journeys of many gifts, and those gifts keep giving because our moms gave us so much, taught us to be grateful and to always count our blessings.

When you count the blessings from your mom, what do you think of first? I'll bet you just smiled. Savor her memory and share it with someone you love. Then, fill your cup with the gift of love delivered innocently in a child's prayer.

GOD BLESS MY MOMMY
"God bless Mommy and Daddy,
God bless Gavin, Cup and Dave,
God bless Nanna and Pappa,
God bless Gumma and Gumpa…"

So went the precious, softly whispered prayer of my then two-year-old granddaughter, giving thanks for people in her life. Faith said that prayer at night, but also randomly throughout the day. I don't know what prompted her prayer, but I paused, listened and gave my own thanks every time she offered hers.

Pushing the pause button long enough to give thanks gets harder as life gets more complicated. We're busy planning, cleaning, solving, feeding and providing transportation for kids going to school, and that's just the first two hours of one morning in my daughter's life as a mom. But Jess has managed to do something very special as a mom: she has taught my grandkids to say "thank you" so well that gratitude easily flows from their lips.

Mom taught me to pray, yet I don't remember the lesson, just the prayers, the places, and the events, like my First Holy Communion. It was easy to pray for good weather, safety when traveling in snow, and of course, for good grades when studying lost out to another television show. While Mom taught me to pray and to count my blessings, her death taught me the biggest gratitude lesson in my entire life.

Losing Mom meant not saying goodbye, and not saying goodbye meant not saying thank you. The letters in *Dear Mom: Remembering, Celebrating, Healing* are reflections of my grateful heart that missed Mom very much. Remembering all I received allowed me to say, "Thanks Mom," and that allowed me to heal.

THE VALUE OF GRATITUDE

We all need healing at different times, in different degrees. Gratitude is an opening to receiving that healing. Maybe that's why Oprah Winfrey said if the only prayer we said was, "Thank you," it would suffice.

Gratitude should flow from us to the world we live in everyday. So often, though, we get busy, too busy to even pause the few seconds it takes to shift into gratitude.

I hope you are on the journey of finding the gifts of your mother's life. Those gifts are the genuine, authentic values that matter. For without the journey, it's impossible to give the gratitude that changes us.

- What are you grateful for in life?
- Have you discovered the blessings of values from your own "Dear Mom?"
- Are you ready to pass them on to help make another's journey better?

If you're a grandmother, you share my joy. I am grateful for every minute I get to spend with my grandchildren. On the trip to the airport at the end of my visit, Faith sat in her car seat and again started her prayer of blessings. But this time, instead of the quiet, whispered voice, she loudly proclaimed: "God bless MY mommy!"

I couldn't agree with her more. God bless all of our mothers—those women we thank today for all the blessings we most likely took for granted, but now treasure and hope to pass on to those little people we love as much as our moms loved us.

PRACTICING GRATITUDE

Giving thanks for the gifts of my mother's life changed my life. Gratitude changes attitudes, fills holes, unveils secrets and opens our hearts.

My daughters both have heard my own gratitude cliché. Frequently repeated, I have said to them, "Don't look at what you've lost, look at what you still have." I learned that the hard way when a fire destroyed my parents' aqua-colored house on the prairie in 1971. And I learned it from losing both of my parents, and most recently, my Aunt Bernice.

Gratitude is a value, and like all values, it is also a skill that we can practice. All you have to do to be changed by gratitude is listen to the prayers of a child.

CHAPTER FIFTEEN

Faith

"It won't hurt this badly forever."
A friend at Mom's funeral.

"Trust God."
Bernice Zenanko

Faith is a simple belief in God. The fact that Mom taught me God exists was one of greatest gifts of her life. However, I have certainly done my share of fighting with Him.

My fight with God began in earnest when Mom died. I felt robbed of Mom by her sudden death at Christmas with no goodbyes and no thank yous. Were you kidding me, God?

The irony was that Mom made Christmas special every year. Christmas celebrates the birth of God's son, and God took my mom just before that celebration. It was simply wrong on so many accounts in my book of life.

CHRISTMAS WITHOUT MOM

"This is your first Christmas without your mom," I said to my dear friend whose mother had passed that year. Surprised, she asked me how I knew. I replied, "I know your mom died this year, and that makes this your first Christmas without her. The first Christmas without your mom is always the hardest of your life."

Her instant tears showed the truth of that grim reality. Life without mom was new enough for my friend, but Christmas without her mom was unimaginable. We became little girls again, confused, wondering where our moms were. Yet, we're now adults, even mothers ourselves, and we thought something was wrong with us. We hid our feelings inside, worried that if we shared our confusion, someone would think us crazy.

Christmas is one of the toughest holidays to face after our mothers died because of what I call "Mom imprints." Moms imprint every aspect of the Holidays—decorating, cooking, shopping, and cards—with their style, creativity, and love. Those imprints are the traditions we cherish, that we likely took for granted because, after all, moms were always there.

HOLIDAY GRIEVING

When my mom died suddenly just before Christmas, I could barely function. The day she died, Mom was crocheting my daughter's Christmas present, a rose-colored afghan. I found the other gifts Mom was making—ornaments for her children—and her hand-written note of who got what. I cut the note apart and gave each of my siblings their gifts from Mom and their names in her handwriting, written in her perfect penmanship, for the very last time.

The pain of holiday grieving intensifies while we're hurting, while we're in such deep pain, as the rest of the world cheerfully sings, celebrates, decorates and enjoys the reds and greens of Christmas. They're festive, and we're not. We used to be just like them when our moms were alive.

The joyful feeling of the holidays will come back. It may come back differently, but it will come back. Let's be good to ourselves. Don't crawl into a hole because our friends and families can be there for us. Moreover, consider writing letters to our mothers.

Writing a letter is one great way to remember and celebrate the wonderful holiday traditions she created. Remember the cookies she baked and frosted? Remember her favorite Christmas music that became our favorite music? Remember when Santa delivered exactly what we wanted, and mom was thrilled for us?

Just write freely and unfettered by worry. Begin to remember more, and write more. When we let our fingers put those holiday memories on paper, we'll have something to clutch to our hearts, to re-read and cry, and that will help us heal.

I did that with my first letter to Mom. I cried, then I re-read it, and I cried some more, and I wrote some more.

Getting the feelings out heals your pain. It's also a great way to create a gift—a memory you may want to share with your family, your children, and someday, your grandchildren. What a great way to honor all the gifts your mom gave you—especially the gift of making Christmas so special.

The letters I shared in *Dear Mom* not only allowed me to remember, celebrate and heal, but also to say, "Thanks Mom."

CHRISTMAS REDEFINED

Losing Mom redefined Christmas for me. I refuse to get caught up in the craziness of unending "To Do" lists that are supposed to make the holiday special. I cannot function within that sphere of busyness. My grief starts on December 5th, the anniversary of her death, and colors the rest of the holiday season with a gray pallor.

Instead, I celebrate the gift of Christmas, decorate a little, and shop less because my husband is the shopper. I take the time I need to write, be with people I want to be with, and enjoy traditions with my own family.

Another antidote to sadness is to identify one of your mom's holiday traditions that you cherish. Consider the influence that tradition has on your life and what it means. Did she make ornaments that still decorate your tree? Did she make salads you can't live without? Did she shop and hide presents in ways you've adopted?

Celebrate your mom's traditions by recreating one of them for friends or family. A woman from Iowa told me that the first Christmas after her mom died, she and her two sisters each brought the same salad to the family holiday dinner—one their mom had made every year for Christmas dinner! What a gift of healing they gave themselves.

Another way to heal is to write a letter. Write to your mom. Or write to your child or grandchild about your mom and one of her traditions. It's an amazing process I used to heal my own pain at mother's death, and it honors the traditions and values of the one who made Christmas special for so many years.

One of my older church friends once said she was going to write a letter about her childhood Christmas celebrations to give to her granddaughters as part of their Christmas presents. She wanted them to know what she valued most about her mom, and how her mom made Christmas special for her as a little girl.

I do know that our stories connect us to our values. When we hear the same story over and over, or for the first time, listen for the values represented in the words, the descriptions of what happened. Listen for values like faith, quality and compassion. None of us will be disappointed to find the wonderful feelings such words bring to our hearts.

CONNECTED THROUGH STORIES

Do you collect things? If so, what kinds of things do you collect? Dishes? Jewelry? Books? Artwork? Furniture?

Antique furniture seems like a large thing to collect. Yet 30 years ago I decided to collect it. My husband eventually got used to the idea, and today my collection includes a secretary, sewing machine, china hutch, dining room table, buffet, trunks, plant stands and a church pew.

I didn't grow up thinking antiques were cool. I grew up thinking my aunt was a bit crazy for hunting for antiques every time she visited us on the farm. Yet, now I am nourished by the memories of Mom serving food on what have become antique dishes. I feel content knowing my antique pew held families in a small, rural church in northeastern South Dakota. And I feel the care of my grandmother's hands as they crocheted the bedspread that kept me warm as a child.

My antiques are connected to the souls of people who used them—or ones like them—in their everyday lives. Bernice and I shared many stories related to antiques, as each piece has a story that connects us to the soul of someone we love.

My secretary, round oak table and sewing machines are all like the ones Mom had. I remember playing with my dad's WWII medals tossed in the secretary, wondering what the stars stood for. I remember making sausage on the old oak table. I can still hear the hum of the old Singer and recall the joy of a new outfit, tailored perfectly for my long arms and legs.

I spoke about finding the gifts of moms and dads to a group of seniors in a Sioux Falls church. I encouraged them to share their stories with their loved ones. They surprised me by sharing them that night.

One man showed us the helmet and gas mask his dad wore in World War I. That's right WW I, not II. He described how his dad marched across France and into Germany where he couldn't get the gas mask on quickly enough and incurred lung damage from mustard gas.

A woman showed us her grandmother's pottery cup with all 12 apostles carved into it. Her grandmother had been an antiques dealer in the mid-1800s in California. Others shared tablecloths, bowls and books. My Aunt Kay showed a spoon that belonged to the first white person born in Day County, where we were both born.

Over and over we heard real stories of real values from real people. That's the kind of authentic story telling young people cherish, and the kind I hope we never lose. Our stories contain values that connect us to our past and strengthen us for the future. The joy we feel in that moment of remembering and sharing our stories is a wonderful reward for creating those connections and helping others grow strong for what lies ahead.

- What stories are in your collection?
- What values do your stories hold? Think about what you've collected and why.
- Can you share your story with your children and grandchildren in a letter, or create a digital video of you telling the story?

Sharing that story with your loved ones brings mom's values to life and offers the next generation their lineage. One of the greatest ironies for me is that Mom's gifts prompted my entire journey of healing that became the book *Dear Mom*.

WHAT ARE YOUR GIFTS?

I wrote my first letter to Mom on the anniversary of her death. My journey of writing letters five years later became the book, *Dear Mom*. I've been amazed how the book encouraged many to remember and celebrate their moms, which lead to healing their pain of loss. What are the gifts of our healing journeys?

We find the imprints of our mother's holiday traditions, the imprints of her entire life—the love and the values that soothe and heal. One woman told me that reading *Dear Mom* was like getting a hug from her late mom. We all need a hug like that at Christmas.

REMEMBER TO BREATHE

I dislike, perhaps even hate, holiday stress, the kind that simmers slowly and produces "The List," complete with "The Timeline." When "The List" is short and time is plenty, I have fun preparing for the holidays. When the inevitable inversion of less time and a longer list occurs, my stress grows.

I hate holiday stress because it takes energy from the joy of relationships I hold dear. Family and friends, in-person visits, cards, e-mails and telephone calls all give greater meaning to my journey.

Like Mom, we all serve by making holiday moments special for those we love. We may do it differently—now using microwave ovens and napkins made by Martha—but we still serve. Our service is our faith in action and a blessing to others.

THE VALUE OF FAITH

Much of the quality of our lives relates to our ability to have faith in something bigger than us, whatever terms you use—God, Higher Power, or Jesus,

When I asked Bernice how she dealt with hard stuff in her life, she said simply, "Trust God." "In God We Trust" is on our currency, and our desire to believe as we please led to the Revolutionary War that gave us separation from church and state, allowing us to choose whatever faith we wanted.

Mom had a simple faith. She cared about faith, but didn't preach it. She lived it by helping others in need, reaching out with what she had like food, clothes and her ability to put together meals for strangers stranded in blizzards.

Unfortunately in life, faith gets complicated. Some use it to justify war. Some use it to polarize America. And some use it to be morally superior to others who do not share their faith.

My mother's faith was simple, her lessons long-lasting.

PRACTICING FAITH

My dad's family came from Norway, a country occupied by
Germany just a few years before I was born. My dad married
my mom, a German Catholic. Thus began my journey of
having a very inclusive definition of "faith" because
opposites fell in love and had the courage to marry anyway.

I saw faith tested on the prairie throughout the year.
Blizzards killed baby calves, the source of income. Dry, hot
wind could damage a crop, and the rain seen as an answer to
prayer sometimes included deadly hail. Yet my parents trusted
that Mother Nature—another term for God—did what she
was supposed to do. It was out of their hands, and they
simply trusted in faith.

Faith is a simple belief in God, reinforced by the simple
beliefs we see in children. In a complicated world, isn't
simple faith the best guidance to living a wonderful life filled
with awe and joy?

Faith says God is in charge, in a very positive way, even when
it's hard to see. That is what Mom taught me long ago.

Faith says the sun will rise in the morning, no matter how
many tears you shed the night before. It's what Bernice
recommended when she said, "Trust God." The simplicity
of that faith is good enough for me.

CHAPTER SIXTEEN

Forgiveness

*"We leave the resolution of the wrongs committed
against us in the hands of the Universe,
releasing ourselves to live a life free of blame."*
Daily OM[2]

"Judge not, that ye will not be judged."
King James Bible, Luke 6:37

"To forgive is divine."
Mom

One of the reasons I have found the gifts of my mother's life relates to forgiveness.

Over the past few years, as I have shared the journey of *Dear Mom* with audiences, several women told me how they wished they'd had a perfect mom. One shared the story of her mother's abuse to her, and a few women painfully rolled their eyes when I spoke about the gifts of a mom.

Life is complicated because all of us have a range of positive and negative emotions with resulting behaviors. I believe at the core, we are good and strive to do well. Yet, we can be not so good sometimes, hurting those we love with our words, thoughts and actions.

An Indian holy man, Ajaib Singh, wrote that within every person are a saint and also a sinner. Depending upon our life circumstances, we develop our habits, frustrations, and addictions. Our own personal pains affect those we love. Yet, I believe most of us never intend to hurt another.

THE NEED TO FORGIVE AND BE FORGIVEN

We all need to be forgiven. All of us do and say things while being unaware of the impact of our words, the pain we caused, or the hurt we rendered. Through the eyes of a child, moms may seem especially mean sometimes.

Moms need to be forgiven. Think about it for a minute. A young woman becomes a mother without a manual. Optimism filled with love meets real life when sleep deprivation leads to exhaustion as she tries to do her best. Add more children, colds and illnesses, then economic stress. Maybe she is a single mom, or only wishing she was sometimes. Life is not easy nor does it meet our expectations or the ideal seen on television and in magazines.

We all react to what life throws at us as well as to things we pick up that weren't even ours in the first place. Moms are no different and certainly not perfect. They are real flesh and blood people who face daunting challenges. I know I was the challenge to my mom and also I was a mom facing challenges. Were you?

Understanding their lives can help us forgive our moms. Forgiveness releases the burden of holding onto the pain caused by another. It also unleashes gratitude. Forgiveness and gratitude allow us to find the good, even in our less-than-perfect life lessons.

We live in an era where blame has become socially approved in America. We easily blame government, teachers and anyone who doesn't meet our standards. This dangerous phenomenon creates victim thinking. Victims can feel totally helpless or not in control of their choices and circumstances. Victims can think that someone or something else always causes the events around them.

Don't be a victim of your mom. Work your way through whatever she did that was not good. Identify what didn't work for you and recognize how you want to be different. Then understand that life really is a journey best lived in the land of forgiveness. Moreover, choose to release the hurts.

I am not minimizing the hurt you may have suffered. Intended or not, hurt is real and has tremendous power to teach. To transcend suffering, we can learn compassion, boundaries, forgiveness, and move on to celebrating our gifts. Forgiveness reminds us that we are works in progress, shaped and influenced by the good and the imperfect of our moms.

JUDGE LESS, HELP MORE

One of my favorite verses in the Bible is "Judge not, that ye will not be judged." I memorized the King James' version of that phrase and thus give away my age. Those words have meant a great deal to me for a long time.

- If we could judge less, wouldn't we be more open and able to receive the gifts of those we love?
- How different would you be—how different would the world be—if you were forgiven, and if you forgave?

Forgive others, including your mom. Pray that others will forgive you, including your mom. Mine is smiling down as I write! Strive to live the life that judges less and understands more.

THE IMPERFECT MOM WITH PERFECT GIFTS

My mom wasn't perfect. Neither am I as my daughters might tell you. I am a member of the Baby Boom Generation. We grew up, sometimes despite ourselves, in a time when we thought we could do anything. Raised mostly by stay-at-home moms, we got all the attention we wanted from those hard-working women.

We were the first generation to grow up with television, which led many of us to expect our mom to be perfect just like June Cleaver. When we compared apron-clad, heels-in-the-kitchen June to mom, well?

When mom couldn't be perfect like June, we knew we could be. So we grew up reading the books, taking the classes, and focusing on becoming the perfect mom our mom wasn't.

Now we're tired. Some of us are grandmothers with colored hair. Some of us have lost our moms. We face life without mom, that imperfect woman, and we find ourselves missing her.

Unlike life on television, my life on the farm included a messy house, mismatched dishes, brownies served directly from the pan, and hair that looked like it had been blown by a prairie tornado. In the midst of that, Mom made mouth-watering dinners, complete with homemade breads, jams and desserts from freshly picked rhubarb. Moreover, all of this was served, of course, on mismatched dishes.

We may not fully appreciate the real value of gifts, especially when they're hidden in the ordinary routines of life. When I reflect on Mom, I find a woman who raised us with her heart filled with love. Hers was real love in action, not a perfect televised version of family.

It's time to give up the fantasy of perfection anywhere in life, especially with moms. Realize the real deal is better anyway. Real moms work hard, strive for simplicity and order in a complicated world, are very creative and resourceful, and laugh to make life better.

When we replace the need for perfection with the need for real, we find what is perfect: the values every mom gives her children. As with antiques, the values of which grow with time, our mom's values become more important gifts to us as we mature. With time, we do realize that mom's values guide us perfectly into the future.

WHEN A WOMAN BECOMES A MOTHER

Every life comes into this world via a mother, and we all truly share this experience. But when does a woman become a mother? At the literal moment of birth? When she conceives? When she tries to comfort what was described as a bundle of joy that now screams loudly?

Becoming a mother is all three…an event, a transformational process, and a journey that never ends.

When a woman becomes a mother she understands how animals in the wild can kill those who attack their young. She knows exhaustion and learns how to minimize her own to care for the baby who can't stop crying. She trusts that her weary bones will rise again the moment a small cry alerts her to suffering that she must ease.

When a woman becomes a mother, she is a mother for life. The love and concern for a child grows like rings on a tree, each year adding more depth and more love, as the child becomes an adult. When a woman holds her child's child for the first time, her life is changed forever again by the sheer, raw delight at the miracle.

When a woman loses her mother, a connection to life itself seems severed. Saying goodbye to the one who gave you life is a most difficult journey. The path is rarely clearly defined and is usually thrust upon us unwillingly.

We don't want to lose our mom and find ourselves fighting through layers of deeper, hidden grief. When we lose our moms, we begin the journey of remembering, celebrating and healing. This process of stripping away all of our emotional debris, all the accumulated junk in our emotional drawers is like birth, painful and joyful at the same time.

We forgive the imperfections, understanding that when a woman becomes a mother, she is still a human being, not a saint. In the process of remembering, we discover the gifts of her life, her values taught to us with her words and recalled as the strangest memories, like I have of Mom's plastic pink flamingos.

The gifts of mothers, even in their imperfect ways, are the strengths of their core values that support our lives. Perhaps the greatest irony is this: When we lose our moms, we find what really mattered most. Such a personal discovery transforms who we are becoming.

Women become mothers, who create life and leave behind simple wisdom and a legacy of values. Those values make our journey great. We can never replace a mom. We can, though, keep her with us forever by finding the gifts of her journey.

- What things about your mom do you better understand after becoming a mother yourself?
- What characteristics about your mom do you see resulting from her own struggles in becoming a mom?
- What can you forgive about your mom that would release negative feelings you might have about her?
- How can you transform any pain into a personal lesson of strength?

PRACTICING FORGIVENESS

I don't believe I need to map out my imperfections or those of my mother as I share this journey. What I do believe is that we all have scars, burns, injuries and wounds that need healing. I am not a psychologist. I believe in taking the journey of healing, and sometimes you need professional help for that process. Get it. Make a positive choice to move through loss, grieving or healing with a compassionate support person. We are far too important to not get the help we need. Then, we move on as best we know how to the journey of finding the best and leaving the rest behind.

I believe that Mom's soul is still quite busy in protecting, loving, reminding me to turn off the oven, to unplug the iron, to be patient with my daughters and to play with my grandkids—even though I'm self-employed and behind schedule.

Mom's authentic gifts made a huge difference in my life. I discovered her gifts because I was looking for them. I have learned to take the best and leave the rest…. and I hope you have, too.

[2] "Burdensome Feelings, Blaming Others" © 2010 Daily Om (April 16, 2010)

SECTION THREE

The Picnic

PAYING MOM'S GIFTS FORWARD

We may run, walk, stumble, drive, or fly,
but let us never lose sight of the reason for the journey
or miss a chance to see a rainbow on the way.
Gloria Gaither

THERE'S NO PLACE LIKE HOME

Nostalgic moments happen on my every journey back to northeastern South Dakota. The endless prairie, divided by fences, trees and fields encourages my soul to come on in and relax a bit. I smile, I laugh, I cry as feelings of life, love and loss move through me when I return to this land where my parents, grandparents and great-grandparents lived and died.

The journey of creating my book, *Dear Mom*, was like that. Every reading and re-reading, writing and re-writing became a journey of memories—the prairie, the family, the old house and new. I smiled, laughed and cried, as feelings became words that described, once again, the gifts and life of a woman of the prairie.

When *Dear Mom* was more than a manuscript, but not quite a book, I returned to my hometown for my aunt's 70th class reunion. On my drive to meet her in Watertown, South Dakota, I realized the importance of my roots to the land. I felt sturdy there, connected to a time that held values I have inherited and tried to make my own.

Each of us has that special place, where deep down inside, we know it's home. It feels right. It feels strong. That's northeastern South Dakota for me, the prairie of my ancestors.

- Where's home for you? Do you associate a specific value with home?
- What word best describes the feeling you experienced at "home"?
- What are some of your favorite memories of that special place?
- Which memories are connected to life with your mom?

Dear Mom was a journey back to that heart for me. I found anew that special place called home and my love for it. I miss the days of Mom's sheets blowing in the prairie breeze. I miss the taste of food that came out of her garden—fresh, delightful and cooked to perfection. I miss the days at the lake when we could splash and cool off and feast on Mom's fried chicken when we were done.

Memories like that make me smile. The journey back in time is a good one. However, sharing the memories is even better. Let's pay our memories forward. Share our values, the gifts from our moms, with those we cherish. Let's speak up, have courageous hearts, and let prairie winds clear the way for future generations.

> *"As the lamp is lit, we begin to see things within us and around us more deeply."*
> Thich Nhat Hanh

God lit my lamp with my book, *Dear Mom,* because finding the gifts of my mother's life through writing helped me heal and grow. The result was seeing the light, so to speak, by practicing the values. Then a passion rose from within me to also pay them forward to my daughters and my grandchildren.

If you had the choice between giving your grandkids a million dollars and instilling in them the values that make life wonderful, which would you choose? For me, the choice is simple. Providing the same core values or personal beliefs that guide my attitude, my communication, my ability to work with people, would be amazing for my grandchildren. Mom's gifts provided the foundation for how I live my life.

If our grandkids' lamps are ablaze, they definitely will see their way to do everything they need to do to succeed. So my goal is to share the treasures of my life, the values handed down from Mom and others who taught me optimism, gratitude, loyalty and other qualities.

My stories that follow share how I pay forward the gifts I found within the pink flamingos!

SPIRITUAL HERITAGE

"This, then, is our true spiritual heritage: not books or ideas,
not monuments of stone or culture,
but the love and sympathy we share for and with all."
Bill Dougherty

Claiming our spiritual heritage is the most important thing we can do today, right now. Our reasons for doing so are simple. We need and deserve the grounding faith of those who came before us. We need and deserve to live the same strength our ancestors showed in their pilgrimage to places we know, as well as those we could never imagine, such as the horrors my dad survived in WWII.

Just as the roots of prairie grasses run deep, so do the roots we all received in the form of values lived by our ancestors. Identifying those values lifts our wings…whether you are a small songbird with a beautiful voice or a giant Canadian goose with a honk heard for miles. Roots give us the lift for our wings, lifts that can't be bought or sold, just practiced.

I have learned to find the values, to live the values consciously, and to make sure I'm sharing them through my work and with the next generation in my family. But to see them as my spiritual heritage was another level I wasn't prepared to take.

Why? People fighting over values fatigue me. I am energized when others share their values and use them to bring out the best in people. People saying one thing and doing another wear me out. I am revived by joyful people practicing their personal, core values as guides to daily living.

Growing up on the prairie meant I had knowledge of two religious views: Roman Catholicism and Lutheran. I didn't know the word Protestant, and I later understood the meaning behind Pre-Vatican II. The irony in my own spiritual journey is that a Buddhist monk, Thich Nhat Hanh, helped me see the values I have been taught as my spiritual heritage in his wonderful book, *Living Buddha, Living Christ*. The values are universal and not to be claimed exclusively by one organized religion.

My spiritual heritage comes from those real people whose arms held me as I later held their hands and shared moments catching fish and baling hay. It comes from real people who survived and smiled despite loss and suffering. It comes from real people whose courage led them to America without ever losing the love for their native Norway.

Those are my people. I once saw them only as my mom, dad, aunts, uncles and grandparents. Now I see them as people who gave me a spiritual heritage cast in real moments lived on the prairie.

WHAT WISE WOMEN DO

> *"I hope the fruits of my labor are ripe*
> *for many generations to come."*
> Donovan Nichols

Wise women review their lineage, not the genetics and bloodlines, but the qualities of heart and soul of their mother lines. In doing so, most of us realize we can choose the best qualities our moms emulated. We admire and model the strength of those who came before us—our mom, aunts, grandmothers, and our "other mothers"…and we say, simply, "Me too!"

- We're strong because of our values.
- We're smart because we've chosen to live them.
- We're wise because we know that living them allows us to pass them on authentically.

It's what we've been waiting for, I believe. This passing along our legacy is a return to what's authentic and right—not judged, just the beliefs known to be our individual truths, and therefore, lived to the best of our abilities.

Every day, listen to the values that encourage optimism, gratitude, kindness and compassion. Live the values of trust, simplicity, resourcefulness and hospitality. Enjoy humor that lightens the load, creativity that helps us see the load differently, and savor the faith that says whatever the load, it will get better.

Claiming our spiritual heritage can lighten the load and remind us to practice our values in every action.

LIKE MOTHER LIKE DAUGHTER
We women do a great job of worrying. Mom worried about me the first time I flew to Japan just two months before she died. When I called to tell her about my trip, she said, "Don't crash into the ocean!" After my eight trips over oceans, I can smile at her warning, knowing it was natural for Mom to worry.

Mom worried about me. I worry about my daughters, and my daughters worry about my grandkids and me. But I worry less than I used to, and I enjoy more, which is a gift of unloading those mental burdens.

Joy replaces concern and worry when I remember to not carry burdens and to release ownership of them to God. Contentment arrives when I remember not to pick them up in the first place.

I used to worry if my children would have all they needed to make their journeys in life great. Now I know they already have it. They came equipped with the ability to learn, grow and figure things out. I've learned to trust them more and stay out of their way while simply helping when I can.

It's a mom thing. It's uncomplicated, but it's deep. The values a mother can give her children cannot be bestowed directly. Mom's values are modeled or demonstrated and reinforced through day-to-day experiences. Moms do it by modeling both good and bad.

In our imperfection and being human, we model both good and bad, as if to empower our children to consider both paths, while encouraging them to choose wisely. The gift of making the journey great is our personal choice, even the choice to have as many re-takes in living until we can turn over the worry.

Choose the positive and hold on to its strength! All the while, know that we choose both good and bad. We can be good; we can be naughty. But naughty or nice, we know our mom loved us, and we'll love our children.

We're just hoping for more nice than naughty!

Finding the values transformed my life and helped me realize the legacy I can share with my daughters and grandchildren.

CUP, EMPTY OR FULL?

> *"I have a simple philosophy: Fill what's empty.*
> *Empty what's full. Scratch where it itches."*
> Alice Roosevelt Longworth

Many people are thirsty in today's world. Their cups are emptied by stressful "To Do" lists, war, the economy, loneliness, loss and even Wikileaks.

In my busy Baby Boomer style, I think I missed some of the good stuff. My cup slowly, gradually emptied as I focused on my career while striving to be a great mom who thought she could do it all. I did accomplish a great deal, and I learned much and shared with my daughters all the travel and learning opportunities available. But as a Baby Boomer grandparent, I think I've grown wiser. Here is what I learned.

I once thought the journey was only results-oriented. Everything I did was focused on goals, and, of course, I had many goals. Goals related to work, career, Toastmasters, finances, education, parenting, and marriage. Directions fueled my goals provided by those lengthy "To Do" lists. If I did the things I had identified as tasks on my "To Do" list, I would reach my goals.

I worked my list, checked off items, and added new items to feel good about my progress. I equated goals with "destination." Yes, I considered the goals to be the destination of my journey, and I kept checking off my destinations, only to add more. Only God knows where I was actually going to end up? In circles?

Then Gavin was born, and the miracle of birth repeated itself in my life. My cup was filled.

THE MIRACLE CALLED GAVIN

Kim, my husband, and I were blessed to be present at Gavin's birth. Gavin almost didn't make it. A difficult labor resulted in lights and bells going off, and my daughter was rushed out of the delivery room into the operating room for an emergency C-section.

At that moment, I was ready to fight God. I paced up and down the hallway outside of the operating room and repeated to God in whispers, "Don't you even think about taking him tonight! Don't you even think about not letting him be born…I don't want to say goodbye to him the way I said goodbye to Mom! Don't you even let him die the way Mom died…don't you even let him die…. We need him in our life!"

Suddenly, the operating room doors burst open. I stopped in my tracks, right behind a pillar, unseen by nurses. As they came through the door, one exclaimed, "Seven minutes start to finish. Damn we're good! We saved that baby!"

I cried. The first miracle happened. My grandson came into the world. My cup was overflowing.

The miracles kept happening as Gavin grew, and my grandmother's eyes saw things more deeply, with more awareness. As Gavin discovered life, I rediscovered it…the joy of seeing the moon and creating a song by that very name with Gavin. Also… the colors of the sky, the rainbow, the simple wisdom of Bob the Builder's "Yes We Can!"

Gavin and I developed our own little rituals. Gavin and his family were moving from Cheyenne to Idaho when he was almost two. As the car pulled away from the curb, I kissed my finger and reached through the car window. He did the same, and our fingers touched…. then I lifted mine, he lifted his, and I said, "Wheeeee!" We have "finger kissed" ever since.

When Gavin's sister, Faith, was born, the lessons of my life with Gavin repeated themselves. What an incredible depth of love I felt holding my child's child. My joys are her toothless grin, sharing the classic *Good Night Moon* and saying good night to everything in her room, and realizing Faith's insight to effectively delay bedtime—again!

Where does that depth of love like Gavin, Faith and I share originate? Had I forgotten the joys of seeing life through the eyes of a child? Did losing Mom and finding her gifts help me see more of the joy in my grandson? Was I just a tired Baby Boomer, ready for new energy?

I believe the love comes from the moms who gave us life and held us in arms that cuddled us to their hearts. Now, I have known that joy in the moments I held my grandchildren. My life was changed forever. Have you experienced this?

Such is the power of love that enhanced my perception from goals to miracles. One result? I now fight a lot less with God.

THE MIRACLE CALLED FAITH

Kim and I were not present for Faith's birth, despite our best efforts. Faith decided to enter this world nearly three weeks ahead of schedule. In fact, I was on my way to a television interview when I got word that she was going to be born that day, and she arrived as I shared about *Dear Mom* with an audience in Sioux City, Iowa.

Jess, her husband, Aaron, and Gavin had just moved to Cedar Hills, Utah, just south of Salt Lake City. Six days later Jess drove herself to a doctor's appointment in Salt Lake City, about an hour's drive. Her doctor informed her she would be giving birth that day. She drove herself home so Aaron could leave work and join her, and just a few hours later, Faith Elizabeth was born.

Almost three weeks later, I met Faith for the first time in the airport. A flood of emotions poured over me as I looked at a baby who looked just like her mother, a face so similar that if our photos aren't dated or easily identifiable by location and date, you cannot discern mother from daughter.

Like mother, like daughter, the miracle called Faith has grown and filled my cup as only a little girl could do!

Life is Like a Picnic

"It just wouldn't be a picnic without the ants."
Author Unknown

I love picnics with my grandkids. I have an antique picnic
basket I packed with our favorite picnic foods and utensils:
peanut butter and grape jam sandwiches, apples, yogurt,
lemonade, spoons, and napkins. Off we went to our favorite
park, playing, sliding, and enjoying the swings and the teeter-
totter. When it was time to eat, we feasted!

Life is like a picnic when we share good food with family and
friends and enjoy the outdoors. What kind of picnic would it
have been if I had packed moldy bread, or a rotten apple, or
sour yogurt, or a soiled napkin? What if I packed the bad
stuff instead of the good?

I have decided to pack the good stuff for my journey to share
the best with my daughters and grandchildren, and to make
sure I take the time to enjoy little things like strawberries with
Faith.

Ten Million Strawberries

I love strawberries, and I have been blessed with bumper
crops. Last summer the yield was 24 jars of freezer jam,
strawberry pies, strawberry shortcake, and a little girl whose
red pants, face and hands offered stained evidence of a day
spent helping pick what she called "ten million strawberries."

My granddaughter, Faith, loves fruit. Each summer when
Faith visits us, I see evidence of her growth and improved
dexterity. Last year we picked strawberries and she ate what
we placed in a bucket. This year she picked, ate, and later
reached for the bowl I tried to hide at the back of the kitchen
counter in hopes of having enough strawberries for the
shortcake baking in the oven.

I shouldn't have worried. With a bumper crop, the supply seems unending. There's enough to pick, preserve and share. After all, as Faith said, we picked ten million strawberries.

Mom grew, picked, and preserved what must have seemed like ten million strawberries in her lifetime. It was easy to take her strawberries for granted because she alone picked, washed, sliced and made them ready to eat. There was no work by us kids, just sore fingers and an achy back for Mom. Hopefully, also the joy of sharing her garden's bounty with her family.

Mom's real gifts, though, were the values that led her to work that hard for us and share her strawberries. Her commitment to quality meant carefully preparing soil, planting, weeding, picking, cleaning and preserving. Her commitment to hard work included hours spent weeding to ensure space for the plants that produced a plentiful crop that fed us. And her generous spirit said there was enough for us and for the birds, since they also loved strawberries.

The core values of a mom that relate to gardening—quality, hard work and generosity—are the essential elements of life we need to practice and live in order to create our own bountiful harvest: a truly wonderful journey that we, in turn, share with our kids and grandkids.

Mom's values remind me of my strawberry patch that simply keeps producing large, ripe berries that we all enjoy. As I picked, bent in positions my back still regrets, Faith would take the berries from my hand and place some of them in the "good berries" bucket. Berries that were waterlogged and moldy from all the rain went into the "bad berries" bucket.

THE YIN & YANG OF STRAWBERRIES

Good berries, bad berries. One becomes the preserves my granddaughter will enjoy this winter and the strawberry shortcake we devour in one sitting. The others don't even come into the house.

Every mom gives their children both kinds of berries. Our job is to take the best and let go of the rest. Moreover, it is our job to forgive mom's imperfections that we might see in ourselves as well, if we look honestly and openly with deeper eyes.

Picking ten million strawberries is hard work. As the temperatures rose, Faith decided to shed her pretty pink sweater. I unbuttoned it, and asked her to put it in the house so it wouldn't get "yucky" outside.

When we were all done, resting on the deck, eating more strawberries, I smiled. My plastic pink flamingo was wearing Faith's pretty pink sweater. A perfect choice made by a little girl on a perfect day picking ten million strawberries.

Life is an amazing journey with great choices. We choose which berries to keep, how many to eat and preserve, and which ones to not even take with us on our journey. Choose to keep the best gifts of your mother's life--and enjoy the sumptuous feast that is yours to savor and share.

SEASONS OF LIFE'S JOURNEY

Birthdays are evidence of getting older on this journey, and I have to confess two things. Since Mom died, you cannot make me feel bad about my age, so I don't detest birthdays. Secondly, I love celebrating my birthday with Gavin and Faith! We create memories together.

When Gavin was three, we celebrated my birthday together. We made my birthday cake, danced and watched the movie, *Madagascar.* We talked, sang and cuddled. And thanks to his patience in walking into yet another bookstore to promote *Dear Mom*, I rewarded him with a pirate play set. We played pirates with a black scarf, eye patch and telescope. Yes, I confess to firing the imaginary gun and enthusiastically proclaiming victory!

My life is enriched every time I'm with Gavin. I'm sure you have your own great memories; some may include your mom with your children. Savor those. Share them. Tell the stories over and over, even if they involve pirates and imaginary guns.

COLOR COMBINATIONS

"We wear the crowns of the queens who came before us…."
Ya Ya Sisters

My granddaughter, Faith, proudly displayed her new creation—a 20" high stack of multiple-colored Lego blocks. When I pointed to each color and asked her to name it, she said, "Red, black, blue, blue, yellow, white, green, green…." through 20+ blocks. Then she looked at me, smiled proudly, and proclaimed, "It's my color combinations!"

I asked Faith what her favorite color is, and without hesitation she said, "Pink!" She's my pink girl. Anything pink is good—balloons, car seat, coat, socks, even her potty chair. When I was Faith's age, I hated pink. Pink was for girls, and I was a tomboy. My favorite color was blue. However, I was my mother's daughter, so she sewed me a pink dress for Easter, which I wore with white gloves. Remember those days? Of course, black shoes were exchanged for seasonally appropriate white shoes since it was spring. Pink and white, and everything nice.

Our life is a journey of taking our favorite color—the one that speaks to our purpose and passion, and savoring the joy it gives.

Memories of our mom can be like those color combinations. We stack them up: mom teaching us to bake, to sew, to be the best we could be every day. Mom teaching us manners, to follow the rules, to be on time. Well, at least she tried!

- Do you remember your mother's favorite colors?
- Can you see the colors of your youth, or of her house today?
- Do you find yourself enjoying the same colors?

Mom's favorite color had to be aqua. The house Mom and Dad built was painted aqua with white trim. The kitchen where she spent most of her time was aqua. The dress she wore to my wedding was aqua. But she also liked pink. The room my sister and I shared was pink, her flamingos in the front yard were pink surrounded by pink and white petunias. My brother's room was blue. I was jealous, and I couldn't wait to move into his room when he went to college, the color being one of the reasons.

The colors of that house are seared into my memory like a photograph. Yet, I have very few photos of it, because a fire totally destroyed that house, photographs and all, 40 years ago.

The colors still speak to me, and now, I even love pink. Especially when it's on a flamingo, or paired up with aqua blue.

THE GREAT ADVERBS OF LIFE

"It is better to travel well than to arrive."
Buddha

Life is a journey to be enjoyed, but it's not only about the end result, like reaching all those goals I wrote. The journey is about how we live it.

The "how" is life's great adverb, and if we don't pay attention to how we are living, we miss the depth and joy of relationships. Our moms taught us the "how." Mom said many times, "It's better to give than to receive." Giving meant sharing, caring and genuinely being there for others. What a wonderful "how-to" for life in any era, on any day.

- The how of optimism: Living with a sense of faith that helps us find solutions and inspires us be our best.
- The how of gratitude: Celebrating and applauding the work of the universe in making the tiniest flower and the tallest waterfalls.
- The how of cooperation: Sharing the effort and working together helps all of us succeed. When we commit to quality we sincerely care to do our best for us as well as those we serve.
- The how of quality: Encouraging their hearts, praising their good grades and helping each other clean a messy bedroom are examples of how we inspire children to do their best at home and in school.

Our cups don't have to be empty. Living by values fills our cups and encourages others to do the same. This journey is incredible and gets better as I see and live the values through Gavin and Faith.

TIME'S A WASTIN!

They had just arrived, my "Little People" who make my life so joyous: Faith, three; Gavin, seven. It was the Saturday night before Christmas, and the 10-hour drive on what Faith calls a "long, flat road" meant unused energy needed a release, just like geysers in their home state of Wyoming.

The lights, the tree and the pile of presents quickened the need for the release, which made giving "Gumma" an early present a good idea. Little Faith took my hand, told me to close my eyes, and as she directed me to the living room, she proclaimed with enthusiasm, "Time's a wastin'!"

My granddaughter has learned well that we have much to do

and need to get it all done. Society rushes us in an approved way: do this, do that, hurry and do some more. It's a socially acceptable success mania, and that's part of what makes holiday grieving so hard.

Grieving during the holidays isn't something that gets wrapped in the perfect paper with a bow that once opened says, "We're done!" Grieving the loss of a loved one means an empty chair, a tradition at risk because the one who created it is no longer there. And when it's your mom, even holiday gatherings with family that were always joyous take on a different tone as families sort out who now does what and who doesn't.

My favorite Christmas memories include Mom's ornaments. Every year she made ornaments for our tree out of yarn, beads and recycled Styrofoam meat trays. This year with an extended visit, there are nine of us here for two weeks. I knew those little geysers needed something to do every day, so each day they received an early present of something to make.

Yesterday's early present was glitter glue, and we used it to re-create Mom's Styrofoam ornaments. Using Christmas cookie cutters, I traced and cut trees, bells, stars, one angel, one gingerbread man, and one duck.

Yes, one duck. I kept all my cookie cutters in one large bag, and when Faith saw the duck, that's what she wanted. So we now had Christmas trees, bells and stars in red, green and blue, as well as a duck with gold glitter...all hanging on our tree.

It was perfect. And I'm sure Mom smiled as much as I did.

Time isn't wasted when you remember and celebrate the gifts of the one you loved and lost, or remember the ones you still have in your life. Time is never wasted on love. I shared my love for Christmas that morning with my daughters over a cup of coffee as we enjoyed the tree and our new ornaments. It was a perfect way to "waste" a little time celebrating our connections and admiring a glittering duck.

After the duck came a bird of a different color. Little hands helped me unwrap the early Christmas gift, but not before I exclaimed with a wide grin, "I wonder what it is?" Faith quickly replied, "It's a pink flamingo!" It was a framed Audubon print, and the process of receiving it was a perfect start to my holiday.

HAPPY BIRTHDAY BETTY!

I recently spoke to a group of women where one woman was named "Betty." I paused immediately and I smiled. No name is sweeter—and no name takes me on my journey faster than the name of my mother, Betty.

That day my mom would have been 82. Instead, she died at age 62, and for the past 11 years, my personal journey has been discovering the nuggets of gold…values that I didn't know I had, or that I simply lived, unaware.

Becoming aware has changed my life, made me more grateful for all I have, and helped me see the goodness in every person. Call me naive, but I will go to my grave believing that we all received the same gifts of values from our moms. Values like gratitude, resourcefulness, kindness and compassion may be buried deep inside, but the seeds are there. The journey becomes a great adventure when we find them, claim them, and live them, to our best ability every day.

"You need not do anything.
Remain sitting at your table and listen.
You need not even listen, just wait.
You need not even wait, just learn to be
quiet, still and solitary.
And the world will freely offer itself to you unmasked.
It has no choice, it will roll in ecstasy at your feet."
Franz Kafka

We're very busy, most of us trying to do too much. I have decided to forego my "To Do" list and replace it with a "To Be" list, which identifies what I want to be every day.
I want to be me, the best of me, and that looks a lot like the best of my mom.

My "To Be" List
- Be kind—even when I am tempted to be a jerk.
- Be compassionate—even when I don't understand. Remember to love more and judge less.
- Be creative—know that I have the resourcefulness to figure out how to do what needs to be done, with a lot of help from God, friends and family.
- Be optimistic—especially on bad days, or when things don't go well. Simply choose to let go, believe and trust. (Deep sigh on this one!)
- Be trustworthy and loyal. Keep things simple. Keep my sense of humor, remembering that the ability to laugh every day keeps the doctor away.
- Be grateful—count my blessings daily, and remember the power of saying "thank you."
- Be cooperative, instead of insisting upon my way.
- And lastly, be committed to quality and hard work, but be the person who chooses each day to make my journey great by being, not just doing.

In case you can't truly forego a "To Do" list, know that I couldn't either. What I have discovered is focusing on what I want to be helps me tackle what I need to do more effectively.

After all, isn't that what our moms tried to teach us?

- What values did you learn from your mom?
- What values guide your journey, make you smile and remember the one who gave you life?
- If you've lost your mom, what values would you think of most on her birthday?
- Would now be a good time to make your "To Be" list?"

As I think of Mom, a wonderful woman named Betty, sweetness fills my soul as the one who gave me life is smiling down from heaven, happy for my journey. Thanks Mom!

WHEN FLAMINGOS RUN FREE

I love taking Gavin and Faith to zoos. We have spent days together exploring exhibits at the Great Plains Zoo in Sioux Falls and the Denver Zoo. Lions, tigers, bears and bugs fascinate them, but it's always special when we get to the flamingos.

One fall day we were taking our usual path in the Denver Zoo. We knew that just around the corner we would see the flamingos, and everyone in my group gets a little excited when they see me seeing flamingos. Faith usually exclaims, "I love flamingos!" My daughter laughs, Gavin gets excited, and I just grin from ear to ear over the live symbol of the gifts of my mother's life.

As we rounded the corner, we were completely surprised and excited to see the flamingos were out of their exhibit, running down the road! Long necks bobbing, looking back and forth, side to side…their exuberant energy screamed, "We're free! We're free!"

We followed them in their excitement, and then saw the zoo keeper who was guiding them to a place where he would feed the birds and answer our questions as we stood within feet of the beautiful pink birds.

I had never been so close to flamingos. The feathers were even more beautiful, the necks even more sleek, and their eyes fascinated me. Perhaps it was my imagination, but the flamingos looked wise, yet crafty, sort of like "we got away!" and now "we'll enjoy this place, too!"

Sort of like Mom. Wise, crafty, sort of like "we'll enjoy and make the most of what life gives us." I doubt Mom ever saw real flamingos. She was content to have the plastic version on metal poles add bold color and character to her front lawn.

Me? I'm glad to have both, and I intend to enjoy all the flamingos I get to see the rest of my life, and make sure Faith and Gavin do, too.

Just as a mother's job is never done, a mother's gifts never end. What are the gifts of your mom? How will you pay them forward?

Losing a mom is one of the hardest journeys in life. Celebrating her gifts transforms the journey from loss into joy.

The love we feel being fully present to all the goodness given us by our moms blesses our every day. May your days be blessed with such goodness and celebration as you find your own pink flamingos!

Appendix

One More Day

MEDITATION TO FIND YOUR GIFTS

Close your eyes for a minute…and imagine a beautiful summer afternoon in the country…. the sun is shining, there's a gentle breeze, and everywhere you look, you see fields of golden wheat, ready for harvest, rippling like ocean waves from the prairie breeze.

You are walking down a road where there is no traffic…. just you, the birds, the sunshine….your heart is heavy because you have lost your mom, and you very much miss the one who gave you life….the one you would call for advice, the one who was always there for you, and now isn't.

Tears come easily as you think about what you miss—her voice, her smile, her cooking, her holiday traditions, her love. As you look down at the grass and listen to the birds singing in the trees next to the road, you see a plain, old, brown bag on the side of the road. You look down, and you see your name on the bag. You pick it up, and you read the tag that says, "A Gift from Your Mom." Surprised, you open the bag, and inside you see a card that says, "Optimism." That doesn't make sense at first…. And you wonder, "Did Mom give me optimism? Was my mom optimistic?" Then you hear your mother's voice when you came from school, mad about something that had happened that day, and you remember with a smile on her face, saying, "Look on the bright side," or "There's a silver lining in every cloud."

You see another bag, and the card inside that bag says, "Teamwork." You shake your head at that one, thinking, "Mom

164

didn't teach me teamwork." Then you remember the way she taught you to get along with your siblings, cousins and friends, and how everyone pitched it to get things done when someone needed help, and how no one was better than anyone else. You smile. Maybe Mom did teach you teamwork after all.

Another bag contains a card that reads "hard work." You understand this one, remembering how your mother worked long hours…. maybe in a garden, maybe sewing your clothes, cooking your food, making brownies for a school event at the very last minute…..

Another bag contains the word "quality," and you remember your mom saying, "If you're going to bother to do something, do it well." Another says "compassion," and you cry as you remember the compassion this woman displayed for so many people and pets in your life…

Another says "gratitude," and you remember your mother telling you to "count your blessings…."

Each new bag contains another word: humor, creativity, simplicity, loyalty…forgiveness, faith and hospitality.

Each plain, ordinary bag holds a gift from your mom…. and as you gather the cards, you begin to realize what the words really are….the values of your mother's life. Values she taught you that you didn't even realize she had given you. And you smile at the irony of taking her for granted—a plain, ordinary mom, imperfect mom after all…and how perfect it is that her gifts come in plain, ordinary, imperfect brown paper bags.

You slowly realize what you have been given: the gifts of your mother's life are really the timeless, authentic values of your life—given to you by the one who raised you with those same values. Tears fall at the same time a smile slowly emerges on your face as you realize what you hadn't known before….those are your values, too. You have become the best part of your mom—and that makes you smile some more.

Now, you begin to understand there's nothing ordinary about the gifts….that these values make you who you are….these values are your strengths…that you are optimistic, that you do work hard, that you are resourceful…..which is why you are going to fold each bag and re-use it, because, after all, that's what your mother would have done!

There's a beautiful patch of grass below a tree next to the road where you sit as the sun descends into a spectacular prairie sunset. As the sun goes down, the beautiful blue sky yields to gorgeous shades of reds and pinks and purples….a flock of geese fly overhead….their honking the only sound you hear as you become aware of a person walking to you on the road, and you realize it's your mom.

You can't believe your eyes as you get up and run to her. She hugs you, says, "I love you." Tears of joy fill your eyes, and all you can say is, "I love you, too—thank you for all the wonderful gifts you've given me." She hugs you again, and simply says, "You're so very welcome. I love you, and I will always love you."

You bask in her love, feeling it deep into your body and soul…time seems suspended. Then as she slowly disappears, you realize the gifts of her love, her life lessons and her values are the most wonderful gifts of your life….that you have been given so much by the imperfect woman who gave you life….that you have everything you need for this journey called life…..and you leave that place to return home, counting your blessings for they are as numerous as the stars that have begun to emerge in the sky, and you realize you have taken the journey of remembering and celebrating the best gifts of your mother's life…..the love, life lessons and legacy of values that will never end.